AVRO
VULCAN

POSTWAR MILITARY AIRCRAFT: 4

AVRO
VULCAN

ANDREW
BROOKES

LONDON

IAN ALLAN LTD

First published 1985

ISBN 0 7110 1548 1

Published by Ian Allan Ltd,
Shepperton, Surrey; and printed
by Ian Allan Printing Ltd at
its works at Coombelands
in Runnymede,
England

For Teresa,
the best wife a Vulcan pilot ever had.

Contents

Cover:
Avro Vulcan B.2 XM607. *Peter R. March*

Half-title
A Vulcan B.2 powers skywards after take-off. Because the earliest B.1s' engines could each only push out 11,000lb thrust, proposals were made in 1957 to fit rocket-assisted take-off gear (RATOG) to ensure adequate performance at smaller overseas airfields. Thus Vulcan Modification No 1 introduced RATOG fixed fittings to accommodate a jettisonable 'Spectre' rocket motor under each wing. However, subsequent Olympus development made such rocket assistance unnecessary, and the Vulcan RATOG concept was abandoned in 1959. *BAe*

Previous page:
Early production Vulcan XA891 showing the new cranked leading edge.

Left:
Vulcan pilots, complete with ejection seat leg restrainers, wait for the AEO to board and carry out his electrical safety checks. The large metal box by the nosewheel contains nothing more sinister than in-flight rations.

Introduction

My final flight in a Vulcan took place on 1 December 1981. No 617 Squadron was due to disband at the end of the year and when it started disposing of its aircraft, the Scampton Station Commander and I ferried XL317 to Cyprus to see out the remainder of its life on the RAF Akrotiri firedump. As I climbed out of the cockpit and down the ladder for the last time, it was like saying goodbye to an old friend. I had enjoyed many memorable moments as a Vulcan captain — the majestic loneliness of low-level missions over the North Canadian wastes, the feeling of elation as the nimble delta out-turned a Lightning fighter yet again, the camaraderie of flying together as a five-man crew. But perhaps the most enduring recollection of all was the 1980 Tactical Evaluation Exercise at Waddington. The order had been given to disperse the Wing to forestall a pre-emptive attack, and in not much more time than it took to strap-in and start four engines, I found myself in the middle of 28 Vulcans positioned on the taxiway awaiting clearance to take-off. I will never forget the sight of the line of bombers, framed in the heat haze of 112 idling Olympus engines and stretching ahead and behind as far as the eye could see. The traffic lights had stopped all vehicles on the road which passed the threshold of Waddington runway, and in the eyes of the motorists who waited patiently must have been that glint of awe and wonder which is always present whenever two or more Vulcans are gathered together. What the onlookers must have thought or feared as we all roared off in quick succession remains a matter for conjecture, but they were witnessing the swansong of the Vulcan force. The RAF will never see its like again for after March 1984 the operational sight and sound of the British strategic bomber was to be no more.

Below:
A Vulcan B.2, its airbrakes fully extended for landing, exudes all the power and majesty for which the delta bomber was universally famous.

1
The Proud Tradition

The Vulcan was heir to a tradition stretching back to World War 1. In 1914 the flimsy aeroplanes of the Army's Royal Flying Corps were little more than airborne cavalry designed to bring back information from 'the other side of the hill' for the benefit of the troops on the ground. Such rudimentary bombing as was undertaken was largely confined to the deposition of the odd projectile over the side in a manner calculated to put aircrew at as much risk as the object of their destructive attentions.

However, as all sides dug in for the duration of the Great War, it was left to the Royal Naval Air Service to point the way forward. After a successful raid on the main Dusseldorf Zeppelin shed, the head of the Admiralty's air department approached Frederick Handley Page and asked him to design 'a bloody paralyser of an aeroplane'. Thereafter the British offensive air effort progressed from attacks on front-line troop concentrations to the rear supply dumps and thence to the factories producing the bullets and shells. It was but a short step from attacking the production lines creating the sinews of war to bombing the workforce that manned the factories in the hope that the enemy population would be rendered either incapable or unwilling to continue the war. By the summer of 1918 as Handley Page's big bombers were appearing, Gen Sykes, Chief of Staff of the newly formed Royal Air Force, noted in a memorandum for the British Cabinet that the aim of the new bombers 'would be to sow alarm broadcast, set up nervous tension, check output, and generally tend to bring military, financial and industrial interests into opposition . . . The wholescale bombing of densely populated industrial centres would go far to destroy the morale of the operatives.' The age of strategic bombing had arrived.

The Independent Air Force, formed on 6 June 1918 under Maj Gen Sir Hugh Trenchard, was the RAF's long range bomber arm and it was the first force to wage war independently of naval or military considerations. Its 10 squadrons attacked industrial and military targets in Germany, and by November 1918 the first four-engined Handley Page V/1500 was ready to carry more than three tons of bombs on the long haul to Berlin.

Although the largest single bomb carried by the Independent Air Force weighed 1,660lb, it has to be said that the RAF was never in a position to prove the effectiveness or otherwise of strategic bombing during the last months of World War 1. Nevertheless the RAF's guiding light, Sir Hugh Trenchard, placed the bomber at the heart of his new Service's philosophy. Trenchard was Chief of Air Staff from 1919 to 1929, and at a time when the two older Services were striving to regain control of aerial forces operating within their spheres of influence, Sir Hugh laid special emphasis on aerial bombing over and beyond the armies and battlefleets as the prime raison d'etre of his independent air arm.

But there was more than self-interest in Trenchard's arguments — the great man firmly believed that attack was the best form of defence. In the last war he had seen the Army stuck in the Flanders mud and the Navy cooped up in Scapa Flow for years. In any future conflict there could be no waiting on the defensive in the skies; the RAF must be in a position to deliver the knock-out blow from the air before the enemy aimed his. As Trenchard told his staff in 1923, 'The Army policy was to defeat the enemy Army — ours to defeat the enemy nation'.

It was advocacy such as this which evoked Prime Minister Stanley Baldwin's famous statement that, 'The bomber will always get through'. Yet although a separate Bomber Command was formed in 1936, the question of *how* the bomber would always get through was left in doubt. The financial restrictions of the 1920s and early 1930s, combined with the need for hasty rearmament in the mid-1930s, forced the British to build up a 'shop window' force of bombers based on deterrence by quantity rather than quality. Thus Bomber Command entered the lists with the Luftwaffe in 1939 with a totally inadequate force of light and medium bombers that could only survive by operating under cover of darkness. Unfortunately, the Command lacked the means of finding and effectively bombing even the largest German targets at night, and the British strategic bomber force was only kept in being until 1942 by the indomitable spirit of its crews.

The arrival of Air Marshal A. T. (later Sir

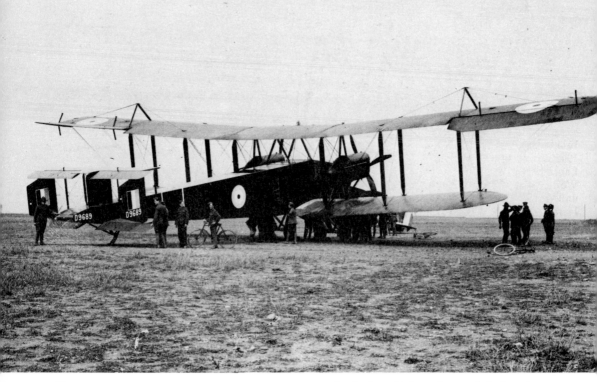

Above:
Handley Page 0/400, stalwart of the Independent Air Force, at Waddington. Forty years later, this grassy field would be covered in concrete to become the RAF's first Vulcan base.

Arthur) Harris to the post of C-in-C did much to improve morale, but it was the introduction of the first of many excellent navigation and bombing aids and the emergence of the four-engined heavy bomber which did most to turn the tide of the strategic offensive against Germany. It is impossible to over-rate the importance of the introduction of new navigation and bombing aids into the Bomber Command inventory. The first was Gee (for Grid) which measured the difference in time required for transmissions from UK ground stations to reach a bomber in flight and displayed the information on a cathode ray tube; from a special Gee grid overprinted on his map, the navigator could then plot his position sometimes to within half a mile. However, aids such as Gee, and Oboe that followed it, were limited in range and their ground emissions could be jammed, so the heavy bombers were also given a self-contained aid called H2S. Some said this stood for 'Home, Sweet Home', others that it resulted from Lord Cherwell's comment on being told about it — 'It stinks' — but either way H2S was an excellent radar device which made use of the fact that water, open country and built-up areas (including individual large buildings) produced distinctively different radar echoes. Unrolling radar maps of the terrain beneath a bomber could be created before the crews' very eyes as their aircraft flew towards its target.

Gee, Oboe and H2S converted strategic bombing from an art into a science but electronic wizardry was only part of the bombing equation; having found the targets, it needed the Lancaster and Halifax bombers plus their skilled and dedicated crews to deliver the crippling punch. By VE Day Bomber Command had dropped a total of 955,044 tons of bombs on targets ranging from city centres to viaducts, and the heavy bomber's impact on the outcome of World War 2 was decisive. Nevertheless, some 55,888 men died on active service in Bomber Command, or 7% of the manpower directly absorbed by the fighting services during the war, and right up to the end of 1944 it was touch and go whether in the war of attrition with the German defences, Bomber Command would emerge the victor or the victim. The British heavy bomber never defeated the enemy fighter in the air, and this was a lesson that the predominantly four-engined, electronically-orientated Bomber Command took very much to heart when it set about planning for the nuclear age.

2
Avro and Roy Chadwick

In a letter to A. V. Roe & Co Ltd in December 1945, ACM Sir Arthur Harris declared that the Lancaster was the greatest single factor in winning World War 2. Even allowing for a bit of understandable licence on the part of 'Bert' Harris, that was not a bad accolade for the firm which 10 years earlier had really only been known for its transport and training aircraft.

Alliott Verdon Roe was born in 1877 and after spells as a surveyor in British Columbia, an apprentice in a locomotive works, a marine engineer and a draughtsman in the car industry, he completed his first full-size man-carrying aircraft in the stable behind his elder brother's surgery in September 1907. The Roe I biplane first took to the air under its own power in June 1908, making 'A.V.' the first man to design, construct and successfully fly a British aeroplane.

By 1909 Roe's younger brother, Humphrey, was running a thriving business at Brownsfield Mills, Manchester, manufacturing elastic webbing and the famous Bull's Eye braces. In January 1910 Humphrey provided support of a different kind to A.V. in the shape of workshop space at Brownsfield to accommodate the new private firm of A. V. Roe & Company. It was probably the first company in Britain to advertise itself as constructors of aeroplanes, and by 1913 the firm had prospered sufficiently to become a limited company and to move to larger premises at Clifton Street, Miles Platting, Manchester.

One employee to make the move to Miles Platting was a young man by the name of Roy Chadwick. Born on 30 April 1893, Chadwick had spent many hours dreaming of 'Argosies in the Sky' in the local Urmston Church choir before persuading Roe to take him on as a draughtsman in the firm's small design office in 1911. Chadwick's unbounded enthusiasm and unsparing energy soon won A.V.'s approval, and Roe 'fathered' him rather than employed him in those pre-Great War days when orders were few and money scarce.

In 1911 the War Office issued its first specification for a military aircraft — a two-seater capable of carrying a 350lb load, climbing initially at 200ft/min and maintaining a height of 4,500ft for an hour, an endurance of 4½ hours and a maximum speed of 55mph. Known simply as the 'Military Biplane', Roe gave it the Type number 500 and it was eventually to lead to A.V.'s most famous creation of World War 1, the Avro 504.

Powered by one of the new 80hp Gnome rotary engines, and possessing an improved wing section, the Avro 504 was to prove itself in war and peace

Below:
A. V. Roe's Type F monoplane, the first aeroplane with a totally enclosed cockpit. This ancestor of the Vulcan, many times removed, made its maiden flight on 1 May 1912 at Brooklands. *BAe*

Above:
A youthful Roy Chadwick beside the Avro 534 Baby. The Baby first flew on 30 April 1919 and it was an early attempt to provide a truly light aeroplane for the private flier. Chadwick taught himself to fly around this time. *BAe*

as well ahead of most contemporary types in both design and performance. 'I candidly confess,' said Roe, 'that it was purely eye and experience which made me settle on the general design,' and this philosophy, combined with natural gifts and a thorough engineering education accumulated over the next 20 years, was to be perpetuated by Roy Chadwick.

The young Chadwick was working on the fuselage and undercarriage of the 504 by the time he was 20, and in 1916 he was ready to design his first bomber, the Type 523 Pike. The Pike was the first twin-engined Avro and, during one test flight of the prototype, the centre of gravity position was so far aft and so tail heavy that the pilot feared he would stall as he came in to land. The situation was only saved by the courage of a young man called Roy Dobson who climbed out of the rear cockpit and along the top of the fuselage to transfer his weight to the front gunner's position. Roy Dobson became Works Manager in 1919 and the two Roys — Dobson and Chadwick — were to combine to even greater effect in the coming years.

Production of 504 trainers continued after the Armistice, thereby enabling Avro to weather the lean years of immediate postwar retrenchment. In fact most of the firm's production and sales in the interwar years consisted of trainers and aero club aircraft such as the Tutor, Prefect and Cadet. Chadwick certainly tried his hand at designing all manner of flying machines from the Aldershot, a massive single-engined bomber, through torpedo bombers to auto-gyros, but they gave him and the company little more than experience. Air Ministry policy was to order a few prototypes of many designs to encourage a host of aircraft firms, and despite the large number of types to come off the

Avro drawing boards, the Antelope and a naval biplane called the Bison were the only non-training Avro military aeroplanes to go into production between the Armistice and the first RAF order for the Anson in 1935.

In 1924, A.V. had bought some land at New Hall Farm near Bramhall where the edge of the Cheshire Plain meets the moors of the High Peak. Known as Woodford, this large pasture with a hangar erected on it would eventually grow into a sophisticated airfield with two runways where final assembly of aircraft and test flying could take place. But in the beginning aircraft were simply towed on their own wheels behind company lorries out to Woodford from the Newton Heath factory.

A.V. left the Company to which he gave his name in 1928, and within a few years the two Roys — Chadwick as Chief Designer and Dobson as General Manager — had taken up the reins. Avro became part of the Hawker Siddeley Group in 1935, and that year the Avro 652 first flew, embodying the new technology of the twin-engined low wing monoplane with retractable undercarriage. The Avro 652A Anson was a straightforward adaptation of the 652 for coastal patrol, and 11,020 faithful 'Annies' were to be built between 1935 and 1952. However, even while the Anson was being developed, Chadwick was devoting the greater part of his working hours to the goal which was ultimately to stamp him as one

Above:
A Lancaster B.1 (Special) of No 617 Squadron releases its 22,000lb 'Grand Slam' bomb over the Arnsberg bridge in Germany on 19 March 1945. This formidable bomb-carrying capacity was only one of the Lancaster's excellent attributes.

of the finest aircraft designers in the world — the creation of a long-range, medium/heavy bomber.

In September 1936 the Air Staff issued Specification P.13/36 for a twin-engined harder-hitting replacement for the Wellington and Hampden. Chadwick's response, known initially as the Avro 679, represented a great step forward for a design team and company that had produced nothing larger than the 19,920lb Ava in 1924 and nothing more complex than the 8,000lb wooden-winged Anson. The 679 not only weighed 20 tons but it also incorporated a stressed skin, all-metal structure and the latest elaborate hydraulic and electrical systems, not to mention new and untried Rolls-Royce Vulture 24-cylinder water-cooled engines of much higher power than any previously used. 'It must (also) be remembered,' said a Chadwick associate, 'that we were commanded to design aeroplanes which would bring the crew back alive, even if the aeroplane was badly damaged or the numbers built had to be reduced.'

The 679 was eventually christened Manchester, and the first aircraft was delivered to No 207 Squadron at Waddington in November 1940. Unfortunately, although much was expected of the Manchester, it proved a major disappointment in RAF service because its large and complex Vulture engines were both unreliable and under-powered. One man who was intimately involved in solving the problem was Stuart 'Cock' Davies. Davies, who owed his nickname to the fact that he stood out as a Cockney in alien northern surroundings, joined Avro in January 1938 as assistant designer to Chadwick. In April 1940 he was appointed experimental shop manager with a brief from Roy Dobson to sort out the Manchester's deficiencies. Time was of the essence for

not only was there a German enemy to be overcome but also there was Avro's great competitor in the bomber stakes, Handley Page, to be considered. 'It was always said in the war,' recalled Davies, 'that the first enemy was Handley Page, the second the Ministry of Aircraft Production, and the third Hitler,' and by 1940 the second enemy was threatening to take over Avro floor space to build Halifaxes unless the North-erners could get their twin-engined bomber right.

The two Roys and Stu Davies spent much of their time in conference with the men on the shop floor discussing how best to create an aircraft that was both efficient in operation and economical to produce, and by the end of July they had decided to replace the two Vulture engines with four of the well-tried and operationally tested Merlin Xs. By adding a fresh outer-wing to house the extra powerplants, Chadwick and his team created the immortal Lancaster virtually at a single stroke, and the first production model was in the air on 31 October 1941.

The outstanding feature of the Lancaster was the large, unobstructed 34ft-long bomb-bay capable of accommodating almost any combination of bombs and mines. The Lancaster's weapon capacity of 14,000lb, or one 22,000lb bomb, plus the addition over the years of radar bombing and navigation aids, made it a natural vehicle for the most glamorous and important Bomber Command raids of the war. Measured in no matter what terms, the Lancaster far surpassed all rivals in terms of range, bombload, ease of handling and surviveability. The statistics tell it all. Some 7,366 Lancasters were delivered to fly 156,000 missions by VE Day, they dropped 608,612 tons of bombs or two-thirds of the total bomb load dropped after the beginning of 1942, and they repatriated 74,000 ex-prisoners of war. It was a record of service that will stand for all time.

Avro's main factory in 1945 was at Chadderton on the outskirts of Manchester, though a wartime shadow factory was built at Yeadon between Bradford and Leeds to swell peak production to 293 Lancasters a month by August 1944. But all creations have to progress or fade away, and the Lancaster eventually sired the Lincoln with its increased wing span and later Merlins to confer better performance and longer range.

However, as the conflict in Europe drew to a close, Avro and Chadwick turned their thoughts to an anticipated postwar air transport boom. A pure transport version of the Lancaster, known as the York to cement trans-Pennine relations, was built at Manchester and Yeadon, but the design office soon progressed to an entirely new passenger type, the Avro Tudor. Built for the North American route, the Tudor was seen as an interim gap-filler for BOAC until the Brabazon and Comet came into being, but the Tudor 1 could only carry 12 passengers. Despite being the first British airliner with a pressure cabin, the Tudor 1 soon fell victim to the ideals set by BOAC for its first postwar airliner, and at the final design conference in March 1946 the Corporation called for no fewer than 343 changes in layout and decor. The writing was on the wall and in 1947 the Tudor 1 was rejected by BOAC as incapable of operating as efficiently as the Lockheed Constellation. Mancunian hopes were then placed on a stretched Tudor 2 to carry 60 passengers, but modifications resulting from the Tudor 1 trials and the weight increase resulting from stretching brought even more troubles in their wake. Simultaneously, Avro was starting work on an anti-submarine Lincoln 3 to be known as the Shackleton. It was a hectic time all round, especially as Yeadon was closing down, and the situation in the Manchester design office was not eased when a specification for a new strategic jet bomber was suddenly thrown into the melting pot.

Below:
The two leaders at Avro standing head and shoulders above the rest — Sir Roy Dobson (left) and Roy Chadwick (right). Roy Dobson became Managing Director in 1941 and was knighted four years later in recognition of his Company's wartime production effort. *BAe*

3
Delta Evolution

Back in 1942 the Ministry of Aircraft Production invited Avro, Bristol, Handley Page, Shorts and Vickers to submit preliminary project designs for an extra-long-range bomber. Fifteen designs were produced in all, ranging in weight from 75 to 100 tons and from tail-first to tailless configurations, and in among them were two conventional design studies of high aspect ratio known as the Avro 681 and 682. Both Avro creations were designed to cruise at 300mph at 20,000ft but they differed in size. The smaller 681 weighed 176,000lb, was powered by eight 2,000hp engines, and was to carry a bomb load of 19,500lb with 8,000 gallons of fuel. The larger 682 weighed in at 220,000lb, was to be powered by 10 engines, and carry 15,000lb of bombs. However, the 682 carried more fuel to go further and had a lower wing loading to fly higher.

Neither the Avro 681 and 682, nor any of the other 13 projects, ever saw the light of day, partly because they were much too large for the runways of the time and partly because the technology of 1942 was just not advanced enough to make them work. Nor was there any real need for them given that bombers of the Lancaster size and genre were perfectly adequate to win the war. But by the end of 1945 two operational advances had taken place which revolutionised the world of aviation — the development of the atomic bomb and the jet engine.

Given that Britain was still a Great Power holding sway over one quarter of the globe, the decision in January 1947 to develop her own atom bomb was inevitable. Unfortunately, despite her scientific contribution to the Hiroshima and Nagasaki bombs, Britain was summarily denied access to US nuclear technology after 1946 by the McMahon Act. Consequently, it would take another six years before Britain detonated her first nuclear device at Monte Bello in 1952, and a few more years after that to perfect her first practical atom bomb called Blue Danube: in the meantime, the RAF resolved to develop the best bomber possible to carry it.

The November 1945 edition of *Flight* described the Lincoln as the 'mightiest bomber in the world', and the type was to remain in Bomber Command service until 1955. However, the Lincoln Mk II,

with its top speed of 305mph at 19,000ft and a range with full 14,000lb bomb load of 2,250 miles, was not an aircraft with which to face the jet age confidently.

In May 1944 a Paper entitled *Future Bomber Requirements* began its sedate peregrination around the Air Ministry. Future bombers, it declared, must be able to reach the enemy's industrial centres and drop the greatest possible weight of bombs accurately on vital targets with the minimum effort and loss. The crucial bombing run therefore was of paramount importance; defensive considerations, even though they might occupy over 90% of the mission to and from the target, were seen as subordinate.

Yet in the words of AVM Sir Robert Saundby, Harris' right hand man at Bomber Command, 'To be successful, a bomber force must not only operate heavily and continuously but it must also be able to maintain at least a small margin superiority over the hostile defences.' This was a lesson that the Luftwaffe should have learned before the Battle of Britain, and Bomber Command became so appreciative of it during its nightly forays over the Reich that it insisted that more thought be given to aircraft defence at the aircraft design stage so that the bomber crews need not worry unduly about defence on their offensive missions.

Height and speed were regarded as the means of salvation in 1946, because the higher a bomber flew the harder it would be to catch, and the faster it travelled the less time it would be exposed to detection and attack by the opposition. The idea of an individual bomber, designed to be superior in performance to anything the enemy might send up against it, dashing in and out of enemy airspace pausing only for as long as it took to drop a nuclear bomb, had much to recommend it to an RAF that was becoming increasingly disenchanted with the massed bomber philosophy of yesteryear. Sheer weight of numbers appeared to confer no great advantage when taking on the Luftwaffe: 'There is no evidence,' said the 1944 *Future Bomber Requirements* Paper, 'to support the theory that using larger numbers of night bombers causes saturation of the enemy's defences. Mosquito losses have been low despite the small numbers in

which they have operated and there is no significant decrease in Lancaster wastage rate when the size of the raid increases. So in night bombing, as numbers do not seem to offer any striking advantage, the decision of optimum size depends mainly on the relative vulnerability of large and small bombers'.

Only a streamlined bomber could fly high and fast, and this meant dispensing with all the turrets which saved not only the aerodynamic penalties of blisters, guns and ammunition but also gunner crew members, associated protective armour, gangways, communications and pressurised life-support facilities to sustain them, and the escape kit to get them out in an emergency. All this seems very straightforward today, but given that the war in Europe had only been over for a year, it was revolutionary to think about sending a heavy bomber twice as far as Berlin with no reassuring guns or armour for protection. The Americans certainly could not bring themselves to make the same break with tradition, and over 30 years later their strategic heavy bombers still carried a rear gunner.

The goal of a large, cleaned-up aeroplane capable of great heights and speeds over long distances demanded turbojet propulsion. As Gloster had been responsible for all jet work within the Hawker Siddeley Group during the war, Avro was initially in the dark about high speed aircraft but the company set to work with a will.

The Vulcan began life as Air Staff Operational Requirement (OR) 229 which stretched industry to the edge of 'the state of the art' by seeking a Lincoln replacement with more than twice the Lincoln's speed and ceiling plus greater range and bombload. The final details of the OR, which later became Specification B.35/46, called for a four-engined jet bomber capable of delivering a 10,000lb nuclear weapon over a still air range of 3,350 miles by day or night from any base in the world. The cruising speed was to be 500kt/575mph (equivalent to Mach 0.873 in the stratosphere) at continuous power over a target 1,500 miles from base. The aircraft had to be capable of carrying a wide range of conventional weapons and it had to reach 45,000ft after one hour and 50,000ft after 2½ hours from take-off. The cruising altitude was to be 45,000ft and it was hoped that the bomber would exceed 50,000ft by as great a margin as possible as fuel weight reduced. Yet in spite of all this, the Specification stipulated a maximum all-up-weight of 100,000lb because the runways of the day could not cope with anything heavier; this limitation was only raised to 115,000lb after pleas from the aircraft industry.

In addition the aircraft had to have an all-weather capability, a high degree of manoeuvrability at height and speed, provision for carrying adequate warning and radio counter-measures equipment, and space for installing tail armament should the argument against carrying orthodox defensive weaponry prove to be invalid. The crew of five — two pilots, two navigators/bomb aimers (who were to take turns at the H2S radar), and a radio communications and electronic countermeasures operator — were to be housed in a single pressure cabin which was to form an ejectable capsule if the bomber had to be abandoned. The whole aircraft was to be designed for large-scale production in wartime with an economic output of at least 500 aircraft at a rate of no fewer than 10 per month. The strategic concept in 1947 therefore was still one of the peacetime RAF acting as an 'expanding nucleus' in time of war.

Roy Chadwick would have been involved in the discussions behind OR 229 and Spec B.35/46. However, towards the end of 1946 he was promoted Technical Director to represent technical policy on the Avro Board and his old job of Chief Designer was given to Stuart 'Cock' Davies. 'I spent the whole of my wartime career as a plumber, not a designer,' said Davies recalling his days in the experimental shop, but when victory was in sight at the end of 1944, he was put in charge of a new design office at Yeadon. After a period when he was solely concerned with York, Athena and Anson developments, Davies suddenly found himself in charge of the Manchester design office where life was becoming distinctly more hectic.

On arrival at his new desk, Davies was immediately drawn into Tudor redesign work demanded by the airlines. For the first two months of 1947 the company was preoccupied with the merger of the Lancashire and Yorkshire facilities because Yeadon was closing, and then there was a national power crisis. On top of this, Chadwick went down with the shingles — as Spec B.35/46, which was issued formally on 1 January 1947, landed on his desk, Davies remembers thinking, '3,000 miles, 500kts, 50,000ft, gross weight of 100,000lb — God help us!' and he was happy to leave it to his Project Office to try and come up with the goods.

The man in charge of the Project Office at the time was Bob Lindley, later to become Vice-President of McDonnell responsible for the Mercury Space Capsule programme. His staff consisted mainly of Mancunians plus the odd Yeadon man brought over by Davies, and fortunately the team had been studying all the German papers they could find on the advantages of swept wings over straight in delaying compressibility, and they were itching to get their fingers around an aircraft with bags of swept-back wing. There was no question of going for a jet Lincoln with a small amount of sweep, and in the beginning the office came up with a conventional tailed aircraft of 45° sweepback at quarter chord. However, the more the team defined its creation, the bigger it got. The trouble with swept wings is that they produce less lift than conventional wings of equivalent size, yet the requirements of altitude demand greater not smaller coefficients of lift. To

compensate for this the Project Office had to increase their swept span, but by the time they had finished they had a design that was going to be of poorer performance and weighing 80,000-90,000lb more than the requirements of B.35/46.

'We were obsessed by this runway requirement of 100,000lb,' says Davies, so it was back to the drawing board in an attempt to combine different degrees of sweep with other means of reducing drag and improving lift such as thinner wings, lower wing loading and lower aspect ratio. However, the speed at which the aircraft was expected to cruise limited the scope of these endeavours, and in the end the structural weight was still so high that it meant sacrificing bomb load to an unacceptable degree. The gloom over Avro resembled a Manchester fog and it was feared for a time that the various specifications of B.35/46 were just too conflicting to be embodied within one airframe.

It took nearly a month to hit on the idea of saving weight by dispensing with the tail altogether. Since a bomber carries its load concentrated around its centre of gravity, and as a swept wing increases longitudinal stability, it came as a bolt from the blue that all the old reasons for having a rear fuselage supporting a tail no longer applied and that it could be deleted once longitudinal controls were fitted to the wing-tips. The Project Office was not ashamed to draw on the tailless research being undertaken by Avro's sister firm of Armstrong Whitworth, but even though this gave an immediate saving in weight and drag the problem remained that the wing itself was still disproportionately large for its purpose and much heavier than required at an estimated gross weight of 137,500lb.

So there was nothing left but to reduce the span. To achieve this by just chopping pieces off the wing was not good enough because it meant decreasing the wing area and thereby upsetting all the carefully calculated factors of wing loading, thinness, and aspect ratio. As the wings got broader and stubbier therefore, Lindley's team kept the wing area constant by filling in the space between the wing trailing edge and the fuselage. By the time the span had been reduced sufficiently to get the weight within acceptable limits while maintaining sweep and reducing tip chord to give adequate induced drag for maximum range, the gap at the back between the short body and the wing trailing edges had been virtually filled in, forming a natural triangular planform resembling the Greek letter delta.

'These three rational stages therefore were the story of how we came to the delta planform "by accident",' says Stuart Davies. 'If ever there was proof that no one could sit down and come up with a brilliant idea it was this — the final shape was

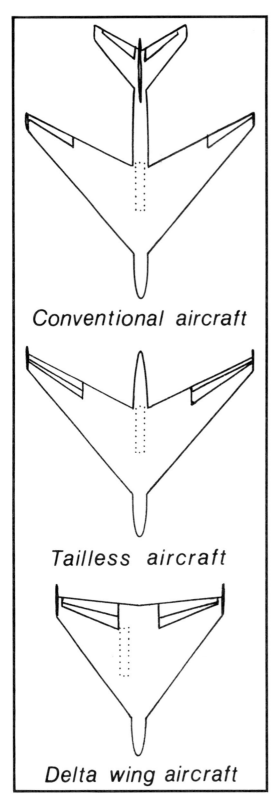

Conventional aircraft

Tailless aircraft

Delta wing aircraft

very much the Project Office (about six chaps) coming up with schemes, rough weight estimates, a quick look at balance, and seeing whether this sort of thing made sufficient sense now to get down to detail. We weren't lumbered with computers in those days so we could do a bit of inspired guessing.'

The idea of using a delta shape was not new. Dr Alexander M. Lippisch had accumulated a wealth of experience with tailless aircraft while working for the German Research Institute for Sailplanes between 1931 and 1937. During the war, in addition to the Me163, he designed the L-13a experimental delta wing aircraft with a leading edge swept back to 60° and powered by a ram jet in the wing centre-section, burning refined coal. However, neither this, nor any other of the delta projects Lippisch and others put through the German wind tunnels, managed to fly before 1945 because of grave lack of stability at low speeds.

Roy Chadwick's imagination had been fired by the German wind tunnel work on delta aerofoils, and while others in 1945 were preoccupied by jet fighters he visualised a 100ft span delta thick enough to contain all the engines and tanks with merely a slight swelling in the centre for the cockpit and bombs. Stu Davies remembers that Avro was tinkering with all-wing aircraft when he joined the firm in 1938 and, 'This was very much the kind of thing Chadwick wanted to do.' Perhaps the great man planted the germ of this idea in his Project Office, for when he returned from convalescence in the spring he liked what his men had produced. 'He was a person who, right from the first time I ever met him, was always obsessed with the idea of the all-wing aeroplane,' says Davies. 'So when he came back and found that his lads had finished up with an all-wing aeroplane by accident, this delighted him more than somewhat. "Right Oh," said Chadwick, "that's the aeroplane," and then he really put his back into the business of selling it.'

It was now March 1947 and time to put some meat on to the bones of the preliminary studies. Avro's thick wing section provided ample space for the proposed blister canopy crew compartment and four Bristol B.E.10 engines which, though superimposed two on each side, were still completely buried close to the centre-line. The bombs, main undercarriage and bulk of the fuel

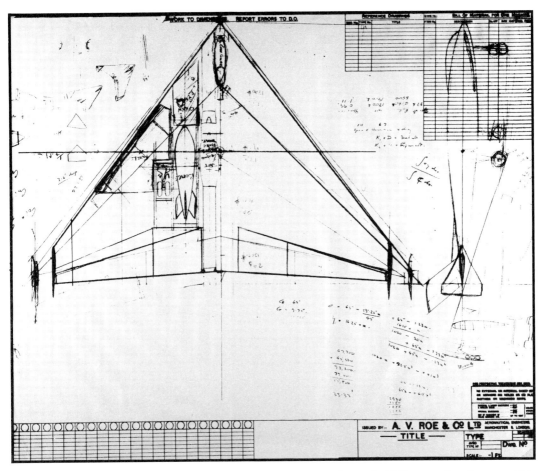

were placed outboard of the engine bays, with the bombs on one side of the aircraft balanced by the fuel on the other. The only things allowed to spoil the pure delta shape were the small swept fin and rudder placed at the end of each wing tip.

The flying controls were to be based on those of the A.W.52, the all-wing tailless aircraft designed by Armstrong Whitworth, and they consisted of double elevons along the wing trailing edge. No flaps were to be fitted as a tailplane would then be necessary to counter pitching moments.

'We never considered any other shape,' says Davies. 'We were obsessed with the idea that the only way to meet this performance was to have absolutely the minimum possible drag which meant the minimum possible skin area. So any idea of hanging engines on pods outside was a sin against the Holy Ghost. It turned out later that this didn't really matter and that you can get the same performance either way, but that's what we thought and what everyone in Britain thought — we all strove to get everything into the minimum possible skin area.'

Consequently the Avro delta was an aircraft designer's dream in 1947 — a wing that was thick enough for the structural engineer yet thin enough for the aerodynamicist. Thin material gauges could be combined with modest stresses yet the wing was thick enough to withstand aeroelastic distortion and possessed a volume of internal usable space nearly double that of a comparable swept-wing aircraft. The large chord at the delta root provided satisfactory damping of pitching oscillations and it also meant that engines, fuel tanks, undercarriage, black boxes and bombs could all be stowed within the wing: this reduced the size of a non-lifting fuselage to a minimum thereby saving on the profile drag of exposed nacelles. Thus the enclosure of everything within the wing, plus the lower wing loading of this large wing area, resulted in a delta shape that was not only very clean and attractive but also one which delayed the drag rise beyond that of a corresponding swept wing aircraft so that it had a greater margin for manoeuvre at height. The only imponderable was the high angle of attack necessary to provide enough lift for take-off and landing, and no one could be sure that the resulting high nose attitude would not result in a stall. But with great gains being promised in range and performance as a result of eliminating the fuselage and tail, it was as good a shape for the future as any customer in the market for an advanced bomber could ask for, and Avro submitted its delta, which it called the Type 698, to the Ministry of Supply in May 1947.

Roy Chadwick would take models of the Avro delta to the Air Ministry to reinforce his point. The effect of this pressure can never be calculated but the Ministry probably gave the delta more support because it came from someone as distinguished as the designer of the Lancaster. Such a pedigree was very important, but tragically Roy Chadwick was killed on 23 August 1947 in the Tudor 2 prototype which crashed just after take-off from Woodford because its aileron controls had been incorrectly assembled. He probably died as he would have wished to finish, at the height of his fame, but as a close colleague stated, 'it was a very sad end for a man who had surely earned the right to relax as a reward for all his achievements and endeavours.'

Roy Chadwick's subordinates looked on him as the complete designer in that he personally supervised every detail of his aircraft on the drawing boards and the shop floor. He lived and breathed aeroplanes, but as a man who was also a fair artist and violinist, Roy Chadwick's epitaph will always be that his creations were more than just flying machines — they were also works of art.

But the days were long gone when any man could summon up a large aeroplane by his individual efforts. Aircraft design and construction may have been a one-man business in the days of wood and bracing wire, but increasing complexity and sophistication made this impossible during and after the war. Now it was a huge team effort, and the greater credit for the Vulcan must be given to Chadwick's team that followed in his footsteps.

For a time it was feared that the Type 698 might be rejected now that the man behind the Lancaster was no longer around to make it work, but the position of Avro's Technical Director was then filled by W. S. 'Bill' Farren, an ex-Director of Farnborough who was much respected in Ministry circles. Stu Davies regarded his Technical Director's experience in the scientific and development field as perfect for Avro, and the two men had a good working relationship. 'I'll turn out the shells, Bill, and you go down to London and fire them,' said Davies, and although if Chadwick had lived he would have fired his own shells, the combined barrage from Farren and Davies led to the decision on 27 November 1947 to accept the Type 698 tender.

But the Avro 698 did not have the British advanced bomber field to itself. Seven companies had originally tendered for Specification B.35/46 and some of the resulting offerings were so

futuristic that Farnborough had to set up an Advanced Bomber Project Group to choose between them. This Group soon found that sweepback was essential to get a speed of 500kt. It also found that the Air Staff restriction on all-up-weight to 100,000lb, and then 115,000lb, was self-defeating in that if wing area could be increased, and wing loading thereby reduced, the bomber could fly higher. Thus, for an extra 40,000lb in weight, the Avro 698 could increase its ceiling by 5,000ft; the Group felt that such benefits were worth the extra tons of concrete needed to make longer runways and the RAF agreed.

Nevertheless, after weighing all the evidence, the Advanced Bomber Project Group had to conclude that 'because of the present uncertainty of basic information, we cannot put all our eggs into one basket. Several designs must be chosen in order to spread the risk'. Thus the Group opted for the Handley Page HP.80 (to become the Victor) because its crescent-wing design was considered to be potentially best in terms of height over the target, together with a tailless delta aircraft of aspect ratio 3, namely the Avro 698, which promised to be more manoeuvrable. The two designs complemented one another, but the aerodynamics of each were still so terribly uncertain that the Project Group had to recommend both in case one turned out to possess some ghastly fault at height that would render it unworkable. In fact the RAF was also to order the Vickers Valiant in April 1948 as a simpler 'insurance' aircraft in case both the advanced bombers failed to live up to expectations.

An Instruction to Proceed — a sort of holding action demonstrating that the Ministry was willing to pay for further development but not yet ready to go so far as issuing production contracts — followed for two Avro 698 prototypes in January 1948, by which time the pure triangle had been much altered. The shape had grown a definable nose during the summer of 1947, containing the crew compartment and radar, and two of the largest circular engine air intakes ever designed had appeared ahead of the leading edge in Gloster Javelin style. Encouraged by Northrop's experiences with the YB-49 flying wing, Avro concentrated initially on losing the fuselage completely inside the wing, but wind-tunnel tests towards the end of the year showed that a reduction in the wing thickness/chord ratio was just as important as wing sweep. This led to the emergence of a fuselage, a not unwelcome sight because it helped prevent the pressure waves from drifting backwards across the wing centre-line thereby upsetting the effective sweepback in the centre-section area. Such a re-arrangement made it impossible to fit the proposed B.E.10 engines in superimposed pairs, so the upper engines were repositioned in the

alongside bays originally designed for bombs. The circular air intakes were still retained at this stage and a stubby rear fuselage appeared between the paired jet pipes. For a time it was proposed to house the bombs in under-wing nacelles but a permanent home was eventually found for the displaced bomb load in the ventral fuselage.

The flying controls for such a novel airframe were an obvious source of concern and discussion.

In April 1948 the idea was to use all-moving wing tips for lateral control with the mechanism housed in the tip fins, but by September the fins themselves had disappeared in favour of a central fin and rudder. A tailplane was not considered necessary, but in case the needs of dynamic stability at high speed proved otherwise, the central fin was considered to be a suitable attachment point should a tailplane have to be added. The elevons were now separated into elevators and ailerons and the engine air intakes became rectangular. At this stage — September 1948 — the designers were finally parted from their 'creation' and Project Designer Bill Willis and his engineers set to work to turn the ideas into reality.

19

4
Mini Deltas

Back in February 1948 the Advanced Bomber Project Group concluded that, 'Energetic research work is imperative to solve hosts of pressing new structural and aerodynamic problems thrown up by the advanced bombers . . . Although we are busily engaged in designing for 50,000ft, experience at such heights is almost non-existent.' Consequently a decision was made to order two full-scale Avro 698 prototypes plus various flying models to explore the whole flight envelope of the revolutionary wing.

After considering various alternatives with the Ministry, it was eventually agreed that Avro's model programme would consist of a single Derwent-engined small-scale delta, the Avro 707, to determine low speed characteristics, and a larger twin Avon-engined delta (the Avro 710) to explore stability and handling characteristics up to the limit of the 698 envelope which was arbitrarily fixed at Mach 0.95 and 60,000ft. Funds were also to be made available for a simplified and stripped full-scale flying model of the 698, the idea being that it would speed up the arrival of the first prototype by ignoring all considerations of operational equipment and merely provide the simplest possible outer shell in correct aerodynamic form.

'These proposals seemed quite logical at the time,' said Stu Davies, 'but as confidence grew, the necessity for the complete programme began to be questioned.' The company recognised that the effort required to design and build the twin Avon model would be almost comparable with that required for the stripped full-scale model, and that to build the one would certainly delay the other. On the other hand the single-engined model, intended as it was mainly to fly at low speed, could be very simple and it was hoped to fly it within a year of starting the design.

By September 1948 the shape of the 698 had been practically finalised, so the twin-engined Avro 710 was tacitly abandoned and replaced by another small-scale model designed for the highest possible Mach number. Thus a new programme was agreed with the Ministry whereby Avro would produce two low-speed 707s, one further high-speed model whose details had yet to be decided, and one unequipped stripped down full-scale 698.

However, by the end of the year the Ministry had concluded that the construction of the last would not only increase expense but might also delay the arrival of the prototype proper. When news filtered through from the USA, where Alexander Lippisch was now employed, that Convair had succeeded in flying the XF-92A transonic research delta, enough doubts were resolved to enable Avro to dispense with the full-scale stripped 698.

The need to save time and money on the low speed 707s was fully appreciated by the Ministry which refused to complicate the issue by specifying an unduly high performance. Maximum IAS was fixed at 400kt and limiting Mach number at 0.85, and the remainder of the specification — E.15/48 — was a model of brevity. The quest for simplicity was reflected in the original intention to build the first 707's wing — which was a one-third replica of that of the 698 — in wood. Stu Davies found it interesting to speculate on the consternation that would have arisen in Manchester if his men had suddenly been called upon to build a wooden aeroplane again after a lapse of so many years; however, a wooden 707 was soon found to be impracticable on technical grounds and the simplest possible metal wing construction was chosen instead, namely a two-spar wing with closely spaced pressed sheet ribs joined to the fuselage by massive pin-jointed fittings. Dick Conner was Project Engineer on the 707, and his team produced a fuselage that was little more than a short, simple welded stub projecting in front, like that which had by this time grown on the Type 698, with a cockpit canopy and nose gear taken from the Gloster Meteor production line. The main undercarriage was that of the Avro Athena trainer, while the engine intake for the 3,500lb Derwent sat on top of the fuselage which also carried the fuel and automatic test recording equipment. It was accepted that this intake was totally unrepresentative and that its ram efficiency would be poor, but this was accepted together with the omission of powered flying controls — the mini-delta had ailerons and elevators operating in exactly the same way as the Chipmunk — because the aircraft was only intended for low speed trials with the emphasis on behaviour at the high angles of incidence required for take-off and landing.

Metal for the first 707 was being cut by the end
of 1948 and the pure delta wing was in its jig early
in 1949. The aircraft itself, serial VX784, was
completed at Woodford in August 1949 and after
preliminary checks and taxying trials, was dismantled and taken by road to the Experimental
Establishment at Boscombe Down on 26 August.
A 20kt cross-wind prevented the planned first
flight on 3 September and the wind did not abate
enough to allow deputy chief test pilot Eric Esler
— known from his RAF days as 'Red' Esler after
Eric the Red — to get airborne until 19.30hr the
following evening. The first flight by a tailless delta
in the UK went without incident, and two days
later VX784 was flown down to the 1949
Farnborough Air Show to take part in the static
display.

Three hours of test flying during September
showed that the behaviour of the type 707 differed
very little from that of any other aircraft, except
perhaps for a longer take-off run. It was therefore
completely unexpected when it crashed near
Blackbushe on 30 September killing Esler. He
appeared to lose control at low speed, thereby
adding fuel to the fire of the Jeremiahs who had
prophesied that deltas were certain doom at high
angle of attack, but it is believed that the real cause
was a fault in the control circuits which locked the
under-wing airbrakes fully out causing the 707 to
stall at low altitude.

Once it was established that the fault was not
inherent in the delta configuration, no fundamental change had to be made to the programme. The
second 707 prototype was then nearing completion
and, as Avro wanted to build something a little less
basic this time as well as learn from Esler's
accident, it was given design time and money to fit
a custom-built ejection seat, completely redesigned airbrakes, and a new elevator nose to
linearise the hinge moment curves. The first of
these changes was pretty drastic since it was not
possible to fit an ejection seat into the original
nose. Fortunately Spec E.10/49, which formalised
the requirement for the high speed model to be
known as the 707A, differed only from its low
speed cousin in calling for an ejection seat and
stressing up to a higher speed of Mach 0.95. As the
design of its monocoque nose plus ejection seat
was practically complete, Avro decided to
accelerate construction of the nose and fit it to the
second low speed 707, which henceforward was
known as the 707B. One change led to another —
a new and longer nose wheel, taken from the
Hawker P.1052, had to be installed because the
now lengthened fuselage made the nose sit up; this
was one of the few occasions when the 707 helped
the 698 programme avoid costly modifications
because the bomber's nose gear could be
lengthened while it was still on the drawing board.
The rear fuselage airbrakes were also deleted and
the wing brakes slightly revised in the form of
narrow plates which swung down on triple arms.
But it was the decision to incorporate a new nose
that considerably delayed the completion of the
707B (VX790) which first flew on 6 September
1950 before going on static display at the

Farnborough Show that same day. Avro's Chief Test Pilot, R. J. 'Roly' Falk, was so pleased with the shiny blue mini-delta which handled like a Moth that he declared, 'Any experienced pilot could handle it after the minimum of briefing'.

Trials with the 707B over the next two years proved conclusively that there was nothing wrong with the tailless delta. Falk found it to be very stable, with no tendency towards the dreaded nose-over-tail tumbling, and he could maintain lateral control well below 100kt until the nose dropped through lack of air speed. The 707 did not even stall at 30° angle of attack, whereas most conventional shapes would have dropped out of the sky around 15°, and Falk looped and vertically rolled it without any problem. Being unpressurised and with manual controls and engine intakes still markedly dissimilar from those of the 698, the 707B could not reflect completely the behaviour of the full-scale bomber, but it was useful in that it reassured everyone that the delta shape worked at low speed, and it did some good when it proved that angling the jet pipe nozzles downwards and outwards would minimise trim changes with power, resulting in the need for a smaller fin on the 698.

During flight tests it became clear that the 707B was capable of higher Mach numbers than the level speed performance would allow, which was limited by the known inefficiency of the air intake. It was felt that if this could be improved without too drastic a change to the structure, the usefulness of the 707B would be very considerably extended, so as a result of tests carried out in the Rolls-Royce wind tunnel at Hucknell, a revised intake was fitted to the 707B in February 1951.

As the 707A fuselage nose had already been married to the 707B, and the latter had been given a new engine intake for faster flight, it seemed that the 707A might not be necessary after all because it promised to do little more for the test programme than add a slight extension to the flight regime. However, the 707B was still a pure delta shape, and by early 1950 the wing and intakes of the 698 had altered so much from the 1947 concept that a body of opinion at Avro pressed for the 707A to be built to prove these features. 'This was quite a big decision to have to face,' said Davies, 'since it was obvious that it would mean complete detail redesign, not only of the wing, but of the centre fuselage including the introduction of the very complications, such as leading-edge air

Left:
The low speed 707B, VX790, with its redesigned longer nose. *BAe*

Below left:
VX790 landing on 28 December 1950 with its brake chute deployed before touchdown. On his first landing, Roly Falk had brought the 707B in at the extraordinary angle of 32° but the mini delta remained perfectly controllable and Falk said that the approach angle did not appear to be so severe from the cockpit. On the second approach, Falk came in at a flatter attitude and released the tail chute about 20ft above the threshold, settling gently and pulling up in a very short space. *BAe*

Below:
VX790 shows its pure delta wing planform. The dorsal air intake for the Derwent engine was just one of the features of the mini delta which were totally unrepresentative of the Avro 698. *BAe*

intakes, that had been so firmly deleted from the original design. It was argued that to do this would mean a major diversion of effort from the 698 and that in any case, whatever the results, it would be too late to influence the design of the 698. Against this it was believed that the extra design load could be handled and that even if the results were too late to alter the design of the 698, they would at least be in time to give guidance on the planning of the first part of the flight programme of the 698, and point to pitfalls and dangers to be avoided. In the end the second school of thought won its point, and in the summer of 1950 detail design commenced on the 707A wing and fuselage.'

The 707A was therefore to be much more akin to the 698 than its predecessors. In addition to the change in wing contours and the incorporation of

the new intakes, it was decided to fix the dimensions and scale in such a way that the ailerons and elevators could now be represented more realistically than on the 707B. But the cockpit was still unpressurised and Roly Falk had to breath a surfeit of oxygen for an hour or so before high altitude flights and then put up with discomfort for short periods at upwards of 40,000ft. Moreover, the Avro test pilots spent hours of flying time, with only two automatic recording cameras covering 24 dials for company, investigating the pitching oscillations of the 707A caused by out-of-phase movement of the manual elevators that had nothing whatsoever to do with the 698. The original 707A, WD280, did not fly until 14 July 1951, and it clocked up 92 flying hours before it was given powered flying controls in May 1952 similar to those of the final bomber. All at once the pitch problem became a thing of the past, highlighting the fact that in many respects the 707 was only a test-bed for itself.

The main trouble with the 707 programme was its lack of co-ordination with the design schedule of the 698 as a whole. It was a marvellous idea in

those days of limited high-speed knowledge to test out theories on relatively cheap models instead of full-scale prototypes, which were then hideously expensive to modify, but it is hard to find any sign of a co-ordinated master plan for feeding information from the 707s into the design of the 698 in time to be of much use. In fact, the whole business got out of synchronisation, with the 707 designers having to alter their models to keep up with the changing shape of the 698 rather than the other way round. Consequently, the first detailed drawings of the 698 were ready to go out to the factory by May 1950, which, even if the first 707 had not crashed at the end of September 1949, would still have given little enough time for model flight test results to be incorporated into the bomber project. The next 707 did not fly until the autumn of 1950, and as for the high speed 707A, metal was being cut for the 698 before that got into the air. In 1952, when the 707A had nearly caught up with its big brother by having power controls fitted, the first prototype 698, VX770, had already been assembled at Woodford from sections transported over from Chadderton. Almost at once the unpleasant discovery was made that the wing of the 707A 'buzzed' increasingly severely as height and speed increased, a fault which was only cured as we shall see later by putting a kink in the leading edge of the delta. By then the 698 was in production and 16 leading edges had to be scrapped, an expensive fate that the 707 programme was supposed to prevent and would have done so had it been timed properly.

However, the little delta reassured everyone from the Government downwards that the triangle could stay in the air. Tip-stalling had been one fear

Below:
WD280, the first high speed 707A, in the air, looking much more like a scaled-down Vulcan. The engine intakes had now been transferred to the wing roots and the dorsal fin had been extended forward. Roly Falk found it to be amazingly manoeuvrable over a very wide speed range, and when he flicked the 707A from one vertical bank to another, he demonstrated not only the high rate of roll but also markedly positive aileron control. Falk's slow rolls with airbrakes extended and nose right up proved that the delta design was an excellent concept. *BAe*

but the 707 appeared incapable of displaying any aerodynamic vices at all. The stall was quite straightforward and very gentle, and while spinning was not a practice to be recommended, Avro did not worry about it overmuch because the stall only occurred at an extreme angle of attack which was impossible to achieve by accident.

With no horizontal stabilising tailplane well aft of the centre of gravity, there was also a fear that the delta would suffer from lack of damping in pitch, but as Roly Falk demonstrated during his immaculate upward rolls and inverted climbs, the delta was extremely stable. Even the pronounced nose-up attitude assumed during landing did not feel or appear out of place to the test pilot. Furthermore, the delta was affected by Dutch roll to no greater or lesser degree than any other aircraft with similar sweepback — the 707 programme however did convince Avro to employ the American expedient of automatic yaw dampers on the 698.

All of which not only made Roly Falk and his associates sleep sounder at night but also kept the Farnborough specialists on Avro's side: but for the 707s the big delta might well have been cancelled before too much money was spent on it on the grounds of unacceptable risk. In September 1951 Air Marshal Sir John Boothman, the Schneider Trophy winner of 1931 and then Controller of Supplies (Air), became only the third man to fly

Below:
The one and only dual-control 707C, WZ744. The 707C went on to be used for some of the first 'fly-by-wire' trials. *BAe*

the 707B, and this 50-year old found it so delightful and docile that he stated, '25 selected pilots must fly it at once.' In Avro's eyes, such enthusiastic support from the RAF was probably worth the cost of the whole 707 programme in itself because it quashed any lingering fears that the delta might be a potential killer.

In 1952 a second 707A was ordered because RAE wanted one for its own purposes, together with four side-by-side dual control 707C conversion trainers for future delta pilots. In the end only one of the 707Cs was built — WZ744. It was put together at Avro's Bracebridge Heath repair and overhaul factory near Lincoln, and when complete it was towed by road to Waddington for its first flight at the hands of Sq Ldr J. B. Wales on 1 July 1953. It was then ferried to Woodford for flight trials.

The other three 707Cs were cancelled but the second 707A — WZ736 — was in the air by February 1953; it was painted orange to add another dimension to the colourful 707 family. But by 1955 the Avro delta had proved itself to be just another aeroplane — 'it is considerably more docile than current swept-wing aircraft of medium aspect ratio,' declared one report — and as the novelty wore off, the 707s were relegated to general research duties such as comparative gun-aiming trials. In 1957 the first 707A was shipped out to Australia for a general programme of low speed research — an ironical end for the 'high speed' 707 — and it now lives in a Melbourne garden after its new owner bought it for a scrap price. The 707B was scrapped at Bedford, but the other 707A and the 707C survive at Cosford Aerospace Museum.

5
Trials and Tribulations

Avro received its first contract for two prototype 698s in March 1949, and by the following September when the first 707 got airborne, the design of the big bomber should have been pretty well frozen. However, it was at this stage that Farnborough threw a spanner into the works. The Royal Aircraft Establishment was the only source of respectable wind tunnel work available to Avro, and Farnborough tests showed that the 698's fuselage was changing the pressure distribution over the wings and engine air intakes from that which the Manchester design office envisaged. In a nutshell, compressibility drag rise would occur on the 698's constant-section wing at lower speeds and at lower heights than had been anticipated, resulting in a degradation of performance. Barry Haines at Farnborough, who did most British work on superficial wings at this time, got hold of Bill Farren and told him that Avro was heading for a fall. 'We had just done all the schemes on where we were going to put the wing root joints, where the undercarriage was going to go, etc,' lamented Davies, 'when along came Haines suggesting that we scrap the whole full-scale wing plan.' The answer lay in sweeping the line of peak section sharply forward over the inner portion of the upper surface of the wing by bringing the thickest part of the section closer and closer to the leading edge. Previously the area of maximum thickness had been in the traditional place around the centre of the wing root — now it was to be thickest at the root leading edge reducing to a minimum at the tip. 'I had a few stiff drinks,' said Davies, 'and thought how to tell Sir Roy Dobson who would have to tell the Ministry that there would be a three-month delay on the job.' Nothing daunted, 'Dobbie' told the Ministry that Avro would sort it all out in a matter of six weeks.

It was now December 1949 and 190 draughts-men had to be put to work virtually to redesign the wing so that the construction of the first prototype would not be too delayed. Not that people minded unduly because the loyalty of Avro personnel to their firm was as intense as the challenge from Handley Page was a spur. 'I remember on one occasion,' said Gilbert Whitehead, who was Project Engineer on the Vulcan, 'going through the factory gates at Chadderton one morning and

not going out again until a fortnight later. It was purely and simply the enthusiasm, the excitement and the busy job that made you forget all about time. Most people involved had the same approach. They were very interesting days.' In retrospect, even though the first detailed drawings of the new wing to go out for manufacture were not issued until May 1950, 'Cock' Davies does not think that the time delay made any real difference. In fact, the change in root design improved engine intake efficiency by a few per cent and the thicker wing root provided plenty of space for future larger engines to fit internally side by side. Thus it came about that Avro produced the first high-speed aircraft whose wing roots were almost as thick as the 9ft diameter fuselage to which they were connected.

This was the crux of the matter. 'The thing that made us change the wing,' admits Davies, 'was not Farnborough, who were a decent set of chaps who didn't bang the table, but the realisation that the day would soon come when we needed to put bigger engines into the bomber, and we needed more room for the holes in the spars and intakes to take the biggest engines anyone could devise. We insisted on keeping the leading edge straight though — we had to keep face in front of Handley Page even though what we were doing thickness-wise was to create a crescent wing.'

In June 1952 Avro was notified that it would receive a contract in August for 25 production models of what Sir Roy Dobson called, 'the most efficient long-range bomber design in the world'. But Handley Page was also given a simultaneous initial contract for 25 Victors and both companies feared that only one type would be ordered into full production after comparative squadron trials. Thus the pressure was on in Manchester to put the first 698 together in time to catch the 1952 Farnborough Show and thereby beat Handley Page into the air. After hastening through ground running and taxying trials, Roly Falk got airborne on 30 August in all-white prototype VX770 that still had no second pilot's seat, cockpit pressuris-ation or wing fuel system.

The 35-minute trip was not uneventful. Falk raised the undercarriage but the nosewheel did not appear to retract, so two other pilots — one in the

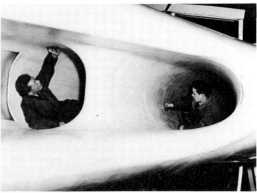

707A and the other in a Vampire — went up for a close look; they confirmed that the leg was up and that the problem lay with a faulty micro-switch. The prototype also lost its secondary main undercarriage fairings because, although the hydraulics had been fully tested on the ground rig, Avro forgot about the flexibility of the wing structure which tore the fairings off like tissue. Nevertheless, Falk recorded after landing that 'even on the first flight I have been able to carry out a variety of manoeuvres, and I am very happy with the aircraft's performance generally'. Roly Falk was later to say that flying the large Vulcan was easier than flying an Anson.

A mere two days later VX770 was flown down to Boscombe where it clocked up three hours' flying time before bringing forth gasps of wonder at the Farnborough Display. The aviation press waxed lyrical over 'the delight of seeing the great white delta wheeling in a blue sky', and the sight of 'futuristic shapes circling on the horizon' gave rise,

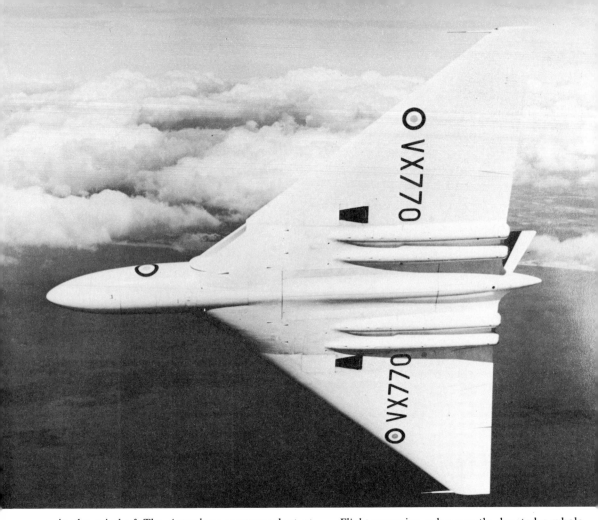

in the mind of *The Aeroplane* correspondent at least, 'to eerie sensations and a feeling that they were extra-terrestrial, manned by species hitherto unknown to man'. The part of the extra-terrestrial species was played by Roly Falk, who swept around the Farnborough circuit showing off the vast white delta triangular wing shape to its best advantage with 'what might be termed abandon'. The undercarriage fairings, which closed the gap in the under surface of the wing between the doors which housed the bogie and the rest of the wing, were not replaced after their loss on the first flight. 'We would never do it today,' says Davies, 'but we decided to fly with the wind blowing around the great holes throughout the Farnborough Show. Every night we had to make modifications to stiffen up the bulkhead which carried the pipework and micro-switches because every day Falk went that little bit faster.' The all-white prototype made five public appearances at Farnborough in all, and each display was climaxed by a neat patriotic Vic formation with the blue 707B flown by Jimmy Orrell on one wing and the red 707A piloted by Jimmy Nelson on the other.

Flight magazine subsequently devoted a whole article to what to call the new bomber and, working from the alliterative base of the Vickers Valiant, came up with all sorts of appendages to Avro such as 'Avenger', 'Apollo' and 'Assegai' (after the Gloster Javelin), before finally recommending Avro Albion. However, the issue was decided by the Chief of Air Staff, Sir John Slessor, who stated that his preference was for a V-class of bombers based on their wing shapes. Handley Page's bomber was to be called 'Victor' and by October 1952 the Air Council had decided to christen the Avro 698 'Vulcan' after the Roman god of fire and destruction. Vulcan was not a new name in aeronautics — it had been used for a Vickers transport in the 1920s — and it did not meet with universal approval. 'I never liked the name,' said Gilbert Whitehead. 'After it was announced I went to look it up in a mythology book and the definition of Vulcan was "misshapen god of war thrown out of heaven".'

Following Farnborough, VX770 was grounded pending modification of the undercarriage fairings and the installation of all the remaining bits and

Left:
VX770 shows off its pure delta wing to the maximum effect. Notice the gaps left by the missing undercarriage fairings. *BAe*

Above:
VX770's appearance at Farnborough in 1952 was greeted by *Flight* as 'a superb example of British design skill, foresight, courage and workmanship. While in no way detracting from the many other magnificent performances, it has stolen the show and opened the eyes of the world.'

Below:
VX770 overflies a Vickers Valiant at Farnborough.

pieces including the second pilot's seat. Roly Falk, for all his flamboyance, was a very cautious character who was not going to fly in a cockpit designed by a committee, so he proposed that he design the Vulcan cockpit personally. Davies thought it was a good idea to give cockpit design responsibility to one man who knew what he was talking about, and Falk's only eccentricity in Davies' eyes was to insist that the Vulcan should not have a conventional spectacle control column. It was so light and easy to fly said Falk that it was going to have a fighter-type stick to get away from

the heavy bomber complex, and this enabled him to close in the whole cockpit. 'At the end of the day,' said Davies, 'the cockpit looked as though it had been designed by one individual because it all fitted, so when the mock-up conference sat it was a brave man who would have stood up and said he didn't like the result.'

Because Falk sat in splendid isolation at Farnborough, and because the flight deck of the production Vulcan with its twin ejection seats close together resembled a sardine can, the myth has grown up that the Vulcan cockpit was originally

Above:
The second Vulcan prototype, VX777, lands at Farnborough in 1953. Notice the visual bombing blister under the nose.

Below:
Delta show-stopper — full scale and mini deltas in delta formation provide an unforgettable climax to the 1953 Farnborough Show. Roly Falk leads the flypast in VX777 with Olympus 100 engines, while Flt Lt W. J. Laidler and Lt A. C. Noble RN fly in 707As on his port wing. Sqn Ldr W. J. Potocki is in the 707B and Flt Lt J. E. Burton is in the 707C on the starboard side, while Sqn Ldr J. B. Wales brings up the rear in Sapphire-engined VX770. *BAe*

designed for one pilot and that the second seat was only crushed in as an afterthought by the RAF. This is untrue because two-pilot operation had been written in from the start. Falk argued that one man could fly the Vulcan and he couldn't understand what the other man was there for, but the RAF retorted that the old days of letting a brand new pilot loose on an expensive bomber had died with the Lancaster and they needed the co-pilot's seat to train captains of the future and to cope if the first pilot was disabled.

Yet Avro's troubles were not over once it got the Vulcan into the air, and it is arguable that the company got the prototype airborne too quickly for its own good. The intention throughout was to power the bomber by four Bristol B.E.10 jets which, in Davies' opinion, 'were the first pieces of decent engineering offered to us at 11,000lb thrust, and the biggest engine you could get hold of for a thing like this has always been my motto, even if it meant not taking a Hawker Siddeley Group engine'. Eventually christened Olympus, the B.E. 10 was specially designed around a minimum frontal diameter (eventually 40in), a long working life, and low fuel consumption for large, long-range aircraft. An Olympus was first run at Bristol's Patchway plant on 6 May 1950, and it had so much potential that in October the Wright Aeronautical Corporation acquired the licence to build it in the USA.

Although initial Olympus trials were carried out at Woodford in a special rig consisting of one half of a Vulcan wing, the engine was still only at the ground testing stage by 1952. Consequently Avro had to look elsewhere for an interim engine for the initial prototype Vulcan flights. At one stage it thought about hanging extra engines under the wing, but in the end chose the 6,500lb Avon as the first interim engine.

The Mk 100 Olympus was in Avro's test rig by February 1953 and the Mk 99 propelled a Canberra to a new world altitude record in May. However, neither was ready for installation in the Vulcan, so after 32 flying hours, VX770 was grounded to allow time for ground testing of the newly completed wing fuel system and to install 7,500lb-thrust Armstrong Siddeley Sapphire 6 engines in place of the Avons to extend the flight envelope.

The next few months saw an intensive period of flight testing covering some 60 flying hours in 57 flights, and during this period the second prototype, VX777, took shape with Olympus 100 engines rated at 9,750lb. This aircraft had a slightly longer nose section to accommodate the extended nosewheel, which in the first prototype had to be telescoped prior to retraction. Finished in gloss white paint, VX777 was the first Vulcan to sport the visual bombing blister, and it flew on

3 September 1953, just in time for Avro to dominate the Farnborough Show less than week later when the company put up a mixed formation of the two Vulcan prototypes and the four surviving Type 707s.

Immediately after Farnborough the second prototype was delivered to Boscombe, but the planned flight testing programme was much delayed by the need to modify the new engines and their fuel control systems. Trials resumed in the spring of 1954 but they did not get far because the aircraft was badly damaged during a heavy forced landing at Farnborough on 27 July 1954. During subsequent repair work, more powerful Olympus 101s, each rated at 10,000lb thrust compared with 11,000lb for production models, were installed together with a number of strengthening modifications.

It was not until early 1955 therefore that VX770 began to explore the high altitude and high Mach number buffet threshold. The 707s had trodden this path already and VX770 confirmed that the straight leading edge planform would bring production Vulcans with more powerful engines unacceptably close to the high Mach number buffet threshold. This had not been apparent earlier because of the lower power output from the interim engines.

'We regarded it as so essential to get flying before Handley Page,' said Davies, 'that we fought tooth and nail to get Avons into the prototype to give Bristol another year to get the Olympus right. Rolls-Royce however were so obsessed by the Canberra that they refused to make any changes to the Avon for us, with the result that we had to make do with Canberra engines with all the accessory gearboxes filling the bomb-bay.' Thus at the order of speeds and heights attainable with 6,500lb Avons, there was not a trace of compressibility stall because the Vulcan was not flying high enough to get into the lift coefficients that were going to lead to it.

The Olympus prototype however confirmed the 707A's discovery that, when 'g' was applied at high level and high speed, a mild high-frequency buffet resulted. Buffeting occurs when the airflow separates from the upper surfaces of the outer wing, and all aircraft, with the possible exception of those with extremely thin wings, suffer from extreme buffeting at high Mach numbers and high angles of incidence. At its worst, buffeting could lead to failure of the outer wing structure, but of more immediate concern to the Vulcan designers was that buffeting cut down range, did little for accuracy on a bombing run, and allowed little margin for evasive manoeuvre before the stall.

A brave face was put on the matter in public. After the Minister of Supply, Mr Duncan Sandys, took control of the Olympus-powered second

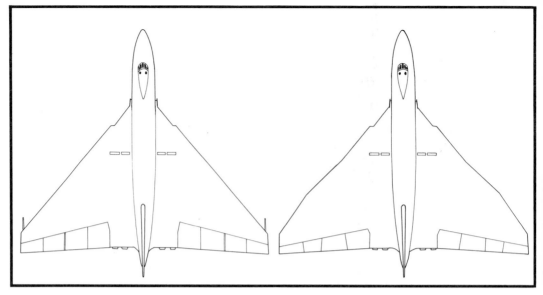

Above:
Plan forms illustrating the differences between the original delta and the Phase 2 kinked outer wing. Both wings carried conventional ailerons and elevators.

prototype for 10min at 50,000ft on 13 March 1954, he reported that, 'We are all much encouraged by the splendid performance of the Vulcan. In test flights in the last few weeks it has shown that it is capable of more than meeting the exacting requirements in both height and speed laid down in the RAF specification of performance. For a large aircraft it is also proving itself exceedingly manoeuvrable at high altitude and speed. These results well justify the adventurousness of its designers and the risk taken by the Government in ordering production before the first prototype had ever flown. The two prototypes which are now being tested have, of course, not yet been pushed, and there is little doubt that the Vulcan still has quite a lot up its sleeve.'

But it was one thing to jaunt about for an hour in a lightly-fuelled Vulcan from Woodford to the Isle of Wight and back; it was another thing altogether to win over the test pilots of the Aeroplane & Armament Experimental Establishment at Boscombe Down, and they were soon to comment scathingly on VX777.

'A preliminary flight assessment has been made on the second prototype Vulcan in 17 sorties totalling 27 flying hours . . . During these tests the aircraft was flown at a mid centre of gravity position and take-off weights of 119,000lb and 130,000lb. The expected operational take-off weight of production aircraft is about 165,000lb.

'The expected cruising Mach number is 0.87M (500kts) and the design Mach number is 0.95M. Above 0.86M a nose down change of trim occurred, which became pronounced with increase of Mach number towards the limit, making the aircraft difficult to fly accurately and requiring great care on the part of the pilot to avoid exceeding the maximum permitted Mach number. This characteristic is unacceptable; the Firm propose to eliminate it in production aircraft by the introduction of an artificial stability device (a Mach trimmer).

'With increase of Mach number above 0.89 the damping in pitch decreased to an unacceptably low level, particularly near the maximum permitted Mach number, and the aircraft was difficult to fly steadily. The Firm propose installing a pitch damper in production aircraft.

'As tested the Mach number/buffet characteristics were unacceptable for a high altitude bomber, but considerable improvement is hoped for with the drooped leading edge and vortex generators. Associated with the buffet were oscillating aileron hinge moments which in these tests imposed severe manoeuvre limitations from considerations of structural safety. . . .

'Making due allowance for the differences in engine thrust and aircraft weight between the aircraft as tested and the production version, the performance, in terms of attainable altitude, was not outstanding. The likely target height with a 10,000lb bomb will only be about 43,000ft with 11,000lb thrust engines, and the high altitude turning performance will be poor. The level of performance is considered to be inadequate for an unarmed subsonic bomber, even under cover of darkness. . . .

'In summary, although the aircraft has certain outstanding features, serious deficiencies are present, particularly in and above the cruising Mach number range, and until these are rectified the Vulcan cannot be considered satisfactory for Service use.'

Stu Davies admits that Avro led itself up the garden path by not getting the right combination of power and wing loading on the 707 earlier, and this attempt to save precious time cost Avro dear. Initially it tried all the standard devices like fences, notches and vortex generators to get more lift out of the 707A, but although most of these conferred substantial benefits at low speeds, the buffeting always reappeared at or below cruising Mach number. Eventually Davies called a big meeting of everyone involved to try and find an answer, including a little chap from the Farnborough High Speed Tunnel Section who didn't say a word for two hours. Then he got up and said simply, 'What you really need is something like this,' and he proceeded to draw a shape that Pete Sutcliffe, then in charge of Avro's aerodynamics office, processed into the Vulcan Phase 2 wing. Basically this consisted of a new outer wing such that in place of the original straight leading edges swept back at 52°, the angle of sweep was decreased by 10° at mid-span but restored again further outboard. The resulting kink gave a 20% increase in outer chord from 78% span to the tip, and a corresponding reduction in loading over the outer part of the wing. The net effect, according to an Avro paper, was 'to reduce the peak lift-coefficient ratio from 1.56 to about 1.3, and this can be regarded as a distinct increase in the incidence at the buffet threshold of about 20%'. The local reduction in

thickness/chord ratio also promised to delay the onset of compressibility effects.

The wing extension also had a thinner, downward-drooping leading edge and was accompanied on early production models by a row of vortex generators above the wing to re-energise the boundary layer. A mock-up of this new wing leading edge was tested successfully on the 707A in 1954 and on the second prototype Vulcan on 5 October 1955, but although the kinks in the previously straight leading edge were located at points that reduced structural alterations to the portion forward of the front spar to a minimum, the special envelope jigging for the leading edge still had to be completely rebuilt and the 16 leading edges already in existence had to be scrapped. It marked the end of the pure triangle shape.

The new — and to many people, more sinister — leading edge arrived too late to be incorporated on the first production aircraft, XA889, which was rolled out at Woodford in January 1955. Painted silver and featuring a new double glass-fibre/Hycar sandwich nose-cone, XA889 was fitted initially with Olympus 101 engines and it first flew on 4 February, 12 months ahead of the Victor. XA889 became the first Vulcan to sport the new wing in February 1956.

On 30 September 1954, Avro received an order for 37 more Vulcans and a year later Roly Falk arrived at Farnborough in the second production Vulcan fitted with nearly all its operational equipment and calmly slow-rolled it before the assembled multitudes. After that nobody disputed the sturdiness, manoeuvrability and fighter-like handling qualities of the new bomber, and when Prime Minister Sir Anthony Eden went for a ride in it after Tuesday's display, the Vulcan had become politically as well as aerodynamically respectable.

What would the great Avro designers of World War 1 and World War 2 have thought of the Vulcan when it was finished? 'I like to think that the Vulcan was as Chadwick would have liked it,' said Gilbert Whitehead who came up under Chadwick and who followed his thinking and approach to problems until he retired as Technical Director at Manchester in 1978. 'Chadwick was convinced that the delta was a good shape to go for and in retrospect, it was a very good shape. It was not the answer to everything by any means — you've got to have compromises — but it was a very good compromise.'

'I think one of the things that would have pleased Chadwick most,' said his successor, Bill Farren in 1956, 'would be to know that we have now made a useful aeroplane out of it, and that we recognise that he started it, not alone, but with the team he built up, who are as proud of the part they have played as he would have been of them.'

As for A. V. Roe himself, who died at the age of 80 in 1958, it is sufficient to go back to his recollections on the birth of the Avro 504. 'Reduction of weight, ease of manufacture, simplification of parts, were among my aims and I felt that the machine would have good flying qualities.' As he looked at the Vulcan in his twilight years, A.V. would have nodded and approved.

6
Vulcan's Forge

Despite its unusual shape and advanced performance, the Vulcan was built along remarkably traditional lines. Structurally, most of the bomber was manufactured from standard grades of high strength light alloy. Although the fin, rudder, ailerons, elevators and folding bomb-doors incorporated magnesium alloy to save weight, this was only because their design was sub-contracted out to Armstrong Whitworth which had gained experience with magnesium in its own flying wing. The undercarriage sub-contractor also used magnesium but Avro fought shy of such experimentation; the company's only excursion into magnesium structures had been with Anson undercarriage fairings which were famous for their disappearing qualities, and if Avro had designed the bomb-doors it would probably have used thinner gauge aluminium instead.

Moreover, although Avro had done much pioneer research into light but rigid bonded metal honeycomb, there was little of it to be found on the Vulcan. Stu Davies waged a personal battle to use it on the bomber but his was a lone voice against those who felt that honeycomb had been developed too late for safe use on the whole aircraft. In the end, the structures men placated their Chief Designer by using honeycomb for such localised areas as the airbrakes and access panels.

As straightforward and well-tried practice was the watch-word of Vulcan construction, the aircraft centred around a two-spar wing structure built on principles which were a logical extension of those employed on the Lancaster. These massive spars, made of orthodox boom and web construction and continuous from port to starboard, bore the main loads in the centre, together with three ribs on either side which partitioned off the engines. Where four holes had to be cut in the rear spar boom to accommodate the powerplants, strengthening was added by four sturdy high-tensile steel rings.

The front and rear centre-section spars formed the fore and aft boundaries of the bomb bay. There was no substantial structure above the weapons bay, major loads being transmitted via strong arches between the inner most axial rib members which also supported the weight of the weapons hung underneath.

Starting at the beginning, sheet-metal parts for the Vulcan were made at the Empire Works in Manchester, ailerons and elevators at Armstrong Whitworth Aircraft at Coventry, fin and rudder at Bracebridge Heath near Lincoln, and the rest in the detail shops at Chadderton. Small parts were then brought together in major component jigs where entities such as the bomb bays and engine intakes took shape; these components were then transferred to the major sub-assembly jigs which were not only more massive than usual because of the soft and unstable subsoil under the Chadderton factory but which also incorporated aluminium alloy members for temperature compensation.

Of these sub-assemblies, the wing centre-section stretching from front to rear spar was the heart and also the largest single piece of the aeroplane. It was built in front and rear portions for convenience and then assembled as a single unit for transportation to Woodford where all the sub-

Left:
Production line of centre section sub-assemblies.

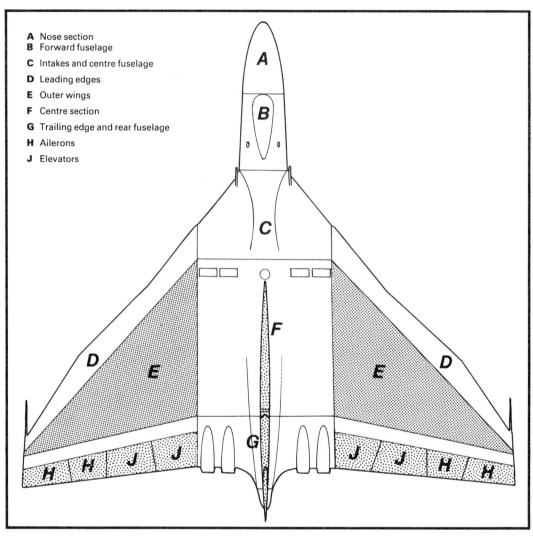

A Nose section
B Forward fuselage
C Intakes and centre fuselage
D Leading edges
E Outer wings
F Centre section
G Trailing edge and rear fuselage
H Ailerons
J Elevators

assemblies were put together to make a Vulcan. Unfortunately, unlike other components involved in the 16-mile journey from Chadderton, the massive centre section measured some 35ft long by 28ft wide by 9ft 7in deep, and this brought problems in its wake. Avro had to liaise with the Borough Engineer to fit numerous hinged lamp-posts on the ring-road around Manchester and through Stockport so that the large centre sections could get by. Later units were redesigned to be split down the vertical centreline into port and starboard halves to overcome this difficulty.

The production hangar was on the west side of Woodford airfield, and when centre sections arrived there, they were initially placed in one of three large centre jigs to check that each of the sub-assemblies was geometrically accurate and within overall tolerances laid down for Service interchangeability. These jigs also held the centre

Above:
The Vulcan airframe broken down into major sections which came together for final assembly at Woodford.

Above right:
Vulcan nose sections take shape at Chadderton.

sections at the correct angle and height above the floor to enable additional manufacturing and installation work to take place. The engine intakes and centre fuselage were then added to the front, and the trailing edge, rear fuselage and fin at the back, whereupon an overhead travelling crane picked up the completed 65ft centre section and placed it on a large trolley for movement up the production line to await union with the outer wings.

The leading edges of the outer wings were

assembled at Chadderton in envelope jigging, a
technique pioneered by Fairey in which the
component is assembled inside a surrounding jig
envelope to attain the highest degree of accuracy
and surface smoothness. The leading edges were a
complete sub-assembly which included the wing
front spar, and the double skin inside the leading
edge incorporated a spanwise duct roughly 0.125in
deep for thermal anti-icing air.

Leading and trailing-edge sub-assemblies were
then transported to Woodford where the main
triangular inter-spar portion of each wing would be
taking shape in one of a quartet of horizontal jigs.
These inter-spar sections were built up principally
from a large number of sheet ribs spaced about
12in apart, and spanwise stringers were then
mounted on the ribs. The box was then skinned
with strips approximately 15in wide extending
from root to tip parallel to the front spar, and the

whole was put together by men working inside the
wing. This was not as difficult as it sounded
because the depth of the Vulcan wing exceeded 6ft
for a considerable distance.

When these preliminaries were completed, the
entire inter-spar rib structure was transferred to
the main outer-wing assembly jig and dropped
between the leading and trailing-edge sub-assemblies. After wing fuel tanks and piping, control
runs and hydraulic equipment were installed, the
complete outer wings were moved on trolleys to
join up with the centre section; they were located
correctly on the wing ribs by means of hand screw
jacks so that height and 'angle of attack' could be
adjusted precisely.

Ahead of the bomb-bay came the fuselage fuel
tanks surmounting the nosewheel bay, at the front
of which was a flat vertical bulkhead. This
bulkhead carried a pair of sturdy vertical members

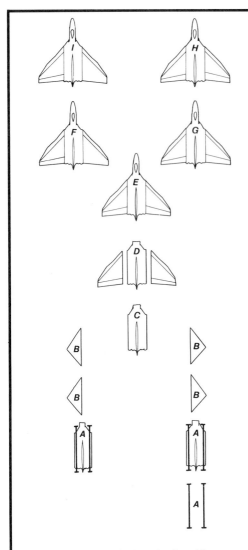

A Three concrete jigs fixed to the floor. These accept the complete centre section, prove it for geometrical accuracy and interchangeability and hold it during further installational work.

B Four horizontal jigs for the triangular outer-wing box between the spars. The edge of the box adjacent to the front spar faces the central walk-way.

C Centre section on trolley awaiting wings.

D Centre section and wings being offered up on trolleys.

E Aircraft in green primer finish, standing on its own wheels and starting functional checks for (for example) fuel, hydraulics, air-conditioning and electrics.

F Aircraft nearing completion, awaiting installation of operational equipment and undergoing pre-flight checks.

G White-painted aircraft undergoing post-flight checks.

H Completed aircraft XH476 in final inspection.

I Completed aircraft XH475 awaiting collection.

through which the nosewheel loads were taken, but more importantly it formed the rear pressure bulkhead of the crew pressure cabin.

Access to the pressure cabin was by means of a removable ladder through a pneumatically-operated underbelly entrance door located just forward of the nosewheel leg. Anyone who scaled the ladder came first to an intermediate 'landing' after which he could either duck forward into the prone visual bombing station, climb a further short ladder to the pilots' seats, or turn back to the line-abreast positions for the two navigators and AEO who sat facing backwards on a raised deck at the rear of the pressure cabin. Rear crews could see out through circular portholes on each side if they had necks like giraffes, and upward and downward-looking periscopes were also provided to allow scanning of the wings and tail.

The entrance door also acted as a dead-air region to enable the rear crew to bale out manually in an emergency, which was a far cry from the crew escape arrangements originally envisaged back in 1946. When the Vulcan specification was first issued, no one had much idea of what it would be like to fly at 50,000ft let alone the effects on a man dangling from a parachute at such rarefied levels. 'The problem of the escape of the crew from a pressure cabin of an aircraft travelling at high speed presents many difficulties,' declared a Farnborough paper on 'The Vulnerability of Future Bomber Aircraft' in February 1948. 'A cabin which may be jettisonable in an emergency appears to offer the most satisfactory solution.'

Thus a jettisonable crew compartment was written into the Vulcan specification. The idea was that, in the event of a serious emergency, the captain would press a button, whereupon the control linkages would sever and explosive bolts would push the pressure cabin clear. Once free from the fuselage, hinged fins would stabilise the tumbling nose before a large parachute came out from behind to lower the capsule, with the crew still strapped in their seats, gently to earth, nose-first, like spacecraft today.

'We sweated blood on that at the start,' recalls Stu Davies.

'We couldn't see how we were going to make it work and we never really got to first base — I don't think we even checked the aerodynamics of the cabin hanging on a parachute. It took a long time

Left:
Stages in the evolution of a Vulcan (not to scale).
Flight.

Right:
Vulcan crew positions and emergency equipment.

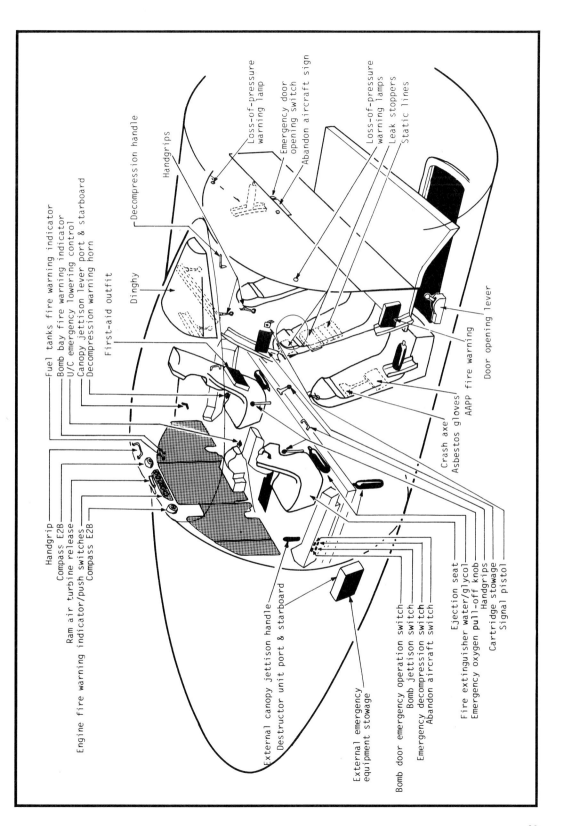

Loss-of-pressure warning lamp
Emergency door opening switch
Abandon aircraft sign
Loss-of-pressure warning lamps
Leak stoppers
Static lines

Decompression handle
Handgrips

Fuel tanks fire warning indicator
Bomb bay fire warning indicator
U/C emergency lowering control
Canopy jettison lever port & starboard
Decompression warning horn

Dinghy

First-aid outfit

Door opening lever

AAPP fire warning
Asbestos gloves
Crash axe

Handgrip
Compass E2B
Ram air turbine release
Engine fire warning indicator/push switches
Compass E2B

External canopy jettison handle
Destructor unit port & starboard

External emergency equipment stowage

Bomb door emergency operation switch
Bomb jettison switch
Emergency decompression switch
Abandon aircraft switch

Ejection seat
Fire extinguisher water/glycol
Emergency oxygen pull-off knob
Handgrips
Cartridge stowage
Signal pistol

Above:
Underwing access door to one of the Olympus engines.

Right:
Bird's eye view of the Vulcan nose showing that the crew's external vision was limited to a narrow windscreen and circular portholes. *Flight*

before we could convince the Ministry that they should abandon the whole idea. If only they'd asked for ejection seats for all crew members from the start, we could have done it. It would have required more canopies but I can't think of any design problem. Unfortunately, in going for tomorrow's technology, we lost out on today's and ended up with yesterday's.'

Thus only pilot and co-pilot sat high up on Martin-Baker ejection seats under a large jettisonable blister canopy which was totally opaque apart from a circular window on each side. As with all the V-bombers, little provision was made for all round vision, the theory being that the structural weaknesses inherent in incorporating windscreens should be minimised in the pressurised environment around 50,000ft. Look-out for defensive purposes was not deemed essential either, at altitudes that were supposed to be well above those of contemporary fighters, so Vulcan pilots were left to view the stratosphere through what amounted to a letter box with bars.

The strange thing about windscreens is that people look through them but rarely at them, and Triplex did a fine job in producing laminated Vulcan windscreens that were not only bullet-proof but could also withstand all the strains imposed by high altitude pressurised flight. Above 40,000ft for example, the aircraft would cool to sub-Arctic temperatures but the windscreen had to be kept clear. This could only be done electrically — power up to 800 watts/sq ft would be necessary for complete de-icing — but vision could not be unduly impaired, so Triplex developed a technique for depositing gold film about .0000002in thick between the layers to maintain almost complete transparency while ensuring essential uniform power dissipation over the heated area.

Below the windscreen the front pressure bulkhead was a simple shallow dish, the lower portion of which was cut off to accommodate the bomb-aimer's window. The cantilevered upper portion of the Vulcan's nose would eventually carry a flight refuelling probe, but in the beginning the main function of the upper section was to support the H2S bombing radar scanner and numerous associated components. The whole nose undersurface consisted of the huge radome, produced by Avro from three fibreglass sheets with two intervening Hycar phenolic sponge layers. The resulting dielectric sandwich radome was one of the largest glass-fibre mouldings ever put into production.

Reverting to the assembly process, the big stalky undercarriage was now put on to allow the airframe to move down the production line on its own wheels. Each Olympus engine was then installed in a separate compartment divided into a number of fire detection and protection zones, and there was a near-rectangular air intake for each pair of engines which divided into individual branches before the front wing spar. Engine installation was a comparatively simple matter via large access doors under the wing.

Having made the Vulcan go, how was it stopped? In the air this was achieved by opening the airbrakes. The original 707B had simple upward-hinging plates, but the 707A pioneered the final arrangement consisting basically of rotating plates mounted on perpendicular arms which motored vertically out above and below each wing. There were three airbrake positions; shut, medium drag (open and slightly rotated), and high drag (fully rotated through 80° to the airflow), the last selection only being obtainable when the under-carriage was down. It was a simple and even crude arrangement — the airbrake arms were motored in and out by little more than glorified bicycle chains — but it was very effective; although relatively small, these brakes added 250% to the profile drag of the clean aircraft.

On the ground, the Vulcan depended on wheels — each of the eight main wheels carried two tyres — and brakes made by Dunlop. Conventional disc brakes with anti-skid Maxaret units stopped the great beast; they were activated by either pilots' foot pedals from two independent hydraulic systems. Trailing edge flaps were not deemed necessary because the great wing stopped itself when pulled up to brake aerodynamically on landing, but an Irvin anti-spin tail parachute was fitted to assist deceleration on short runways or if the hydraulics failed.

Design and manufacture of the flying control surfaces, which got the Vulcan on and off the ground in the first place, were subcontracted to Armstrong Whitworth. Imputs to the duplicated elevators and ailerons came from the pilots via normal push/pull rods with appropriate bell cranks and levers, but manual strength could not overcome high subsonic airflows and so powered flying controls for each surface were designed and produced by Boulton Paul. Both ailerons and elevators were divided into inner and outer portions, each of which was operated by its own power unit to provide complete duplication. Thus if one elevator power-pack failed, the remaining three elevator surfaces would continue to operate: such a failure would have no effect on aircraft performance though the controls would feel heavier to the pilot.

Flight trials on the 707A and the first Vulcan prototype had pinpointed the need for an autostabilisation system, and so a yaw damper, a pitch damper and a Mach trimmer were designed and fitted to the second prototype in November 1955. Avro went to exceptional lengths to prove all the Vulcan systems right down to fitting a g-sensor into the automatic Mach trimmer circuit to isolate the system in the event of a runaway. Thus at this stage in production, the embryo Vulcan went through an extensive ground test programme, of which Stuart Davies was very proud, to check powered flying controls, hydraulics, pressurisation and air conditioning, engine installation and fuel system.

The production Vulcan carried some 33 tons of fuel internally, and there was concern in the early design stage as to the effect on the bomber's centre of gravity as this fuel was burned in flight. These fears were aggravated by what was known as the 'Ten Per Cent Rule' proviso of Spec B.35/46 which said that if an aircraft suffered a fuel tank strike, it should not affect more than 10% of the total capacity at any one time. The only way round this was to distribute the fuel around a number of separate small volume tanks, and at first Smiths Instruments proposed an elaborate control system whereby the tanks would feed in proportion to signals received from the fuel contents gauges. Apart from the frightening complexity of this scheme, it was felt that it might prejudice the reliability of the fuel gauges themselves, so a simpler but equally effective solution was devised, based on an electric motor driving a few cams that switched pumps from full to half speed cyclically to keep the fuel centre of gravity constant throughout the flight.

This fuel system typified the approach of Davies and his team to the Vulcan. 'We had such a party

with pressurisation on the Tudor that we said that the Vulcan will be foolproof. The crew will set a knob and from then on they won't have to touch it.' A Chief Designer on a 'super priority' bomber such as the Vulcan carried a great deal of clout in putting his policy into practice. For example, the original electric motors on the Boulton Paul flying controls were found to overheat, so Davies demanded Rotax motors instead. 'I was told that I was interfering with Ministry policy, so I said they'd better change their policy then. In those days you could do that, and in the end Rotax provided 160 components on each Vulcan B.1.'

As a hangover from his experimental shop days, Davies set a firm timetable and then thumped the table to make sure it was met, but he could only get away with this policy because the Vulcan was never made too complicated.

'It was an old joke that Avro aircraft were built by simple folk for even simpler folk to fly, and we knew that there was nothing wrong with the Vulcan that we couldn't fix by putting a tailplane on it. However, the real reason why we knew we had a winner was the fundamental simplicity of the thing. I could demand that the second prototype be built within 12 months of the first because the

Below:
Height and Mach number performance of XA889 as plotted by Boscombe Down during Vulcan acceptance trials in the spring of 1956.

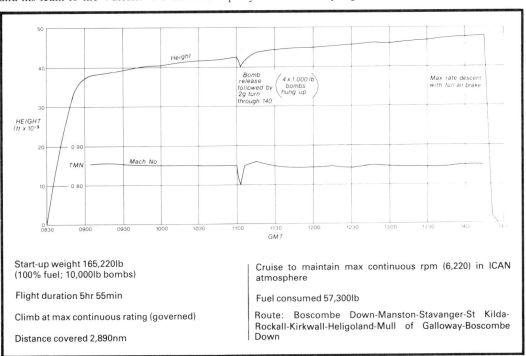

Start-up weight 165,220lb
(100% fuel; 10,000lb bombs)

Flight duration 5hr 55min

Climb at max continuous rating (governed)

Distance covered 2,890nm

Cruise to maintain max continuous rpm (6,220) in ICAN atmosphere

Fuel consumed 57,300lb

Route: Boscombe Down-Manston-Stavanger-St Kilda-Rockall-Kirkwall-Heligoland-Mull of Galloway-Boscombe Down

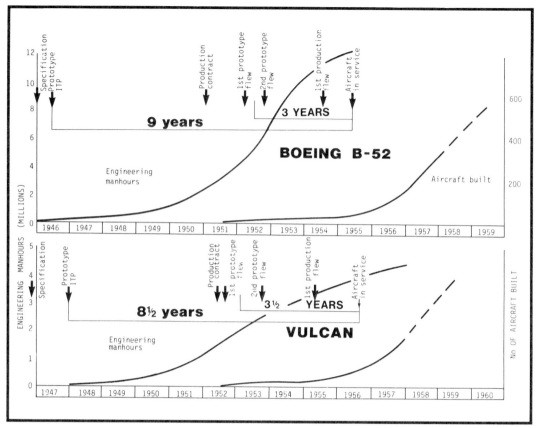

Comparison of Avro Vulcan and Boeing B-52 development programmes. The curves show the total engineering man-hours expended plotted against date; the term 'engineering' covers the whole process of research, design and development but excludes manufacture. The effective starting point has been taken as the receipt of the Instruction to Proceed.

systems were simple enough for us to learn enough about the plumbing and electrics from the first prototype to scrap practically the entire issue and re-do it all again on the second.'

Davies' philosophy was reflected throughout the firm — 'Simplicate and add lightness was our motto,' recalls Gilbert Whitehead. 'Some people think it's clever to be complex but it's a darn sight cleverer to be simple. It's very difficult to get a simple solution to a lot of problems but it's worth striving for.' This approach was certainly appreciated by the RAF when it came to fly and maintain the Vulcan, and it played a big part in keeping Avro consistently ahead of Handley Page in the advanced bomber race because the latter often made things too complicated with the Victor. The net result was a tribute from the Under-Secretary of State for Air who said that the Vulcan 'has probably had the minimum amount of teething trouble of any aircraft introduced in the RAF over the last 10 years.'

Each completed Vulcan was made ready for flight testing in a hangar at the other side of Woodford airfield, and at the appointed hour it was flown for the first time still wearing its green undercoat of standard etching primer. After flight testing, the Vulcan was brought back to the head of the assembly line and given two coats of glossy white anti-radiation paint. It was subjected once more to thorough checks and then delivered to the expectant customer.

A single Vulcan B.1 cost around £750,000 and for this the RAF received a bomber consisting of 167,063 separate parts (excluding engines), 410,300 nuts, bolts, washers and rivets, enough metal sheeting to cover 1½ football pitches, 9,362ft of tubing, 2½ miles of rolled sections and 14 miles of electrical cabling. When it was all put together to make the first production Vulcan, XA889 with its 11,000lb Olympus Mk 101 engines was delivered to Boscombe Down for acceptance trials in spring 1956. Initial CA Release (Release by the Controller, Aircraft for operational use) came on 29 May:

AEROPLANE AND ARMAMENT EXPERIMENTAL ESTABLISHMENT BOSCOMBE DOWN

Vulcan B. Mk 1
(4×Olympus 101)

Trials for initial C.A. Release

A & A.E.E. Ref: AAEE/5701,n/1.

Trials Period: 26th March-17th April 1956

Tests have been made on the first production Vulcan B.Mk.1 to assess the type for use by the Royal Air Force in the medium bomber role. The trials programme was completed in 26 sorties totalling 48 hrs 15 mins flying time.

During these tests the aircraft was flown over the full centre of gravity range and at take-off weights up to a maximum of 165,220lb.

The first production Vulcan, XA 889, was representative of service aircraft in all respects save those of operational equipment, automatic pilot, the rear crew stations and certain items of cockpit layout. The aircraft incorporated the drooped leading edge outer wing with vortex generators, the longitudinal auto-Mach trimmer, the pitch damper and revised airbrake configuration . . . These modifications have successfully overcome the unacceptable flying characteristics exhibited by the second prototype in the preliminary assessment carried out by this Establishment, and when all stability aids are functioning the Vulcan has safe and adequate flying qualities for its primary role as a medium bomber.

The RAF received its first Vulcan in July 1956, and Avro was justifiably proud of its achievement in getting such a radically new bomber into service in eight and a half years. The firm's Technical Director, Sir William Farren, was not slow to underline the point:

'During the past five or ten years it has often been stated, in Parliament and the Press, that we design and eventually produce good aircraft, but that for some reason we take far too long about it . . . The first news which the British taxpayer gets about a new aircraft is generally when it flies at the SBAC Display at Farnborough. If it is something really new, and puts up a good display, a fairly early entry into service is taken for granted — not only by the public, but also by the RAF. It is, therefore, understandable that there is puzzlement, and even dismay, when several years pass before the type is really at work in service . . .

'There has recently been released remarkably comprehensive information about the main weapon of the USAF Strategic Air Command, the Boeing B-52, and a comparison can now be made between the times taken on the B-52 and Vulcan taking into account the differences between them, and the resources available.

'For each aircraft two prototypes were built. Both B-52 prototypes flew in 1952. The first Vulcan prototype flew in 1952 and the second in 1953. For comparison of the "flight development" times it is sufficiently accurate to reckon from a date midway between the first flights of the two prototypes. The period between this date and the delivery of the first aircraft is 3 years for the B-52 and 3½ years for the Vulcan.

'Although the two aircraft are in certain essentials very similar, there are large and obvious differences between them. The B-52 is much larger, and is more complicated both in construction and in equipment. Its empty weight is about double that of the Vulcan. Experience shows that, for aircraft of similar essential characteristics, engineering man-hours are approximately proportional to the weight, rather than to the size. The scale of man-hours for the Vulcan has been chosen as double that for the B-52, and the similarity of the two curves is striking.

'There is a sudden rapid rise in the B-52 man-hours early in 1952, evidently due to the great urgency of the production programme, for which a preliminary order for 500 was placed a year earlier. The number was later raised to about 600. At the present time about 300 have been built.'

Sir William was correct to mention this point because Vulcan orders by 1956 were only a tenth of those for the B-52. On the other hand, Boeing's design and engineering staff numbered some 5,500 whereas the Manchester design office numbered no more than 700 in 1949. A total of 39,500 drawings absorbing 1,467,000 drawing office man-hours were required from the start of the Avro 707 programme to completion of the basic Vulcan, but the important fact from the prestige point of view was that the B-52 took nine years between receipt of its Instruction to Proceed and arrival into service, whereas Avro needed only eight and a half years to produce the Vulcan. Without doubt the Americans had the facilities to build their bombers in hundreds over a relatively short time, but as Sir William concluded, 'When allowance is made for the differences between the B-52 and the Vulcan, and for the relative strength of the resources deployed, there is *no significant difference between the "overall" and "flight development" periods of the two aircraft.*' It was positive proof that when it came to research, design and technological ability, the British in general and Avro in particular were second to none.

7

Higher and Further

Despite Avro's achievement in creating the Vulcan from scratch, the re-jigging of the Phase 2 wing inevitably delayed emergence of the bomber in any appreciable numbers. The first batch of aircraft was employed on development and trials duties and although the RAF received its first Vulcan on schedule when XA897 was handed over to No 230 Operational Conversion Unit (OCU) at Wadding-ton on 30 July 1956, it was a symbolic gesture; immediately afterwards XA897 was sent back to Boscombe Down to join XA895 in completing service acceptance and intensive flying trials. Furthermore, XA897 was returned to Woodford in August prior to setting out on 9 September on a diplomatic flag-waving mission to New Zealand via Melbourne (the venue for the Olympic Games that year). As a proving trip for the Vulcan and an

advert for British global might, the flight was an undoubted success, but as XA897 returned home from 'Tasman Flight' on 1 October it struck a field of Brussels sprouts 2,000ft short of Heathrow runway. The shattering blow to the undercarriage damaged the flying controls, and the captain, Sqn Ldr Donald Howard, DFC, AFC, was help-less. The VIP welcoming party on the roof of the Central Terminal Building at Heathrow could only gaze in horror as the delta reared upwards out of the murk 'like a giant ray leaping from the ocean'. Two staccato cracks followed as Howard and his co-pilot, Air Marshal Sir Harry Broadhurst, C-in-C Bomber Command, ejected, and the great aeroplane keeled over with mind-numbing slow-ness to hit the intersection of Nos 1 and 4 runways. It bounced for a further hundred yards, a booming explosion rent the air, and the Vulcan came to rest in a billowing mass of smoke and flames killing all the rear crew.

Consequently, No 230 OCU did not receive an aircraft it could truly call its own until XA895 and XA898 arrived at Waddington in January 1957. Having completed Intensive Flying Trials, the OCU began crew training on 21 February 1957.

Each Vulcan carried a crew of five — captain, co-pilot, navigator/radar, navigator/plotter and air electronics officer (AEO) — and No 230 OCU

Below:
XA897, the first Vulcan to make an overseas flight, at Ohakea, New Zealand, after establishing a point-to-point record between Hobart and Christchurch at an average speed of 634mph. XA897, standing beside a diminutive Vampire of No 75 Squadron RNZAF, is seen in the early Vulcan silver paint finish — notice the red, white and gold City of Lincoln shield on the fin. XA897 was soon to embark on its fateful and fatal return to London Airport. *BAe*

initially trained half a squadron or 4-5 crews at a time. Selection of Vulcan aircrew was given special emphasis and in the beginning it was jokingly said that you needed 2,000 flying hours just to pull the chocks away. All crew members had to hold 'above average' flying assessments and from the outset all Vulcan aircrew were commissioned officers. New crews were declared Operational once they proved their worth on a squadron, and as bombing and navigation accuracies improved, a crew would be promoted first to Combat and then Select status. It was originally intended that Combat and Select crews would serve together for five and a quarter and seven and a half years respectively, and to provide further incentive the designation Select Star was added for the crème de la crème. Select and Select Star designations were later changed to Senior and Command, but either way these classifications were awarded only to crews who were consistently good over a period of years.

Flt Lt John Pack was on No 1 Vulcan course as a co-pilot, and he was sent the following letter beforehand by the CO of the OCU, Wg Cdr Frank Dodd:

'Dear Pack,
    You will, no doubt, have been told by now that you have been selected as a member of Number 1 Vulcan Operational Conversion Course . . . I hope that you will enjoy the course

Above:
The second operational crew to graduate from the Vulcan OCU board their No 83 Squadron aircraft. Left to right: Sqn Ldr Donald 'Podge' Howard (captain), John Pack (co-pilot), Roy Hansard (Nav Plotter), 'Slim' Pocock (Nav Radar) and Jock Wilson (AEO). In those early days, captains had to be rated 'above average', possess at least 1,750 first pilot hours, and have previous four-engine as well as Canberra experience. Thus John Pack, although he had been a QFI on Vampires and held an 'above-average' rating on Canberras, could only be a co-pilot because he had no four-engine experience and had not yet amassed 1,750 first pilot hours. He became the first Vulcan captain who did not possess the magic 1,750 total when the RAF ran out of these stalwarts.

as much as we, after months, almost years, of waiting are enjoying the prospect of getting down to work in earnest. Our experience to date with the Vulcan has been most encouraging. It is a business-like aircraft but of gentlemanly behaviour, and I am sure you will like it as much as we do . . .'

Flt Lt Pack's first flight in a Vulcan took place on 28 March 1957 with Wg Cdr Dodd. As they left the ground, Frank Dodd relieved the artificial feel thereby making the control forces very light, and handed over control. It was the first time John Pack had flown a big jet and his initial impression was 'how bloody easy the Vulcan was to fly'.

Above:
Vulcans of No 101 Squadron in formation. From the arrival of XA901 on 4 April 1957, all production Vulcans were finished in an overall gloss white paint, produced by Cellon, which was reflective to give protection against nuclear flash. *BAe*

Right:
Olympus 101 engine undergoing servicing at Waddington. Although the Olympus 101 produced 11,034lb of static thrust, it only weighed 3,650lb and an official report on this reliable and efficient engine stated that it set 'a standard of handling at altitude which has never been equalled by any other turbine engine'. The Olympus was such a good design that it was subsequently developed to power Concorde. *Rolls-Royce*

Pack's captain was to be Sqn Ldr Howard, survivor of the London Airport crash, and together with the other graduates of No 1 Course they left No 230 OCU at the end of May 1957 to form 'A' Flight of No 83 Squadron, also at Waddington. The second OCU course completed the No 83 Squadron complement, but the Squadron had to exist on aircraft borrowed from the OCU until its first Vulcan — XA905 — was collected from Woodford by Howard's crew on 11 July 1957.

The next OCU courses went to No 101 Squadron which re-formed at Finningley on 15 October 1957. Coincidentally, the last aircraft from the 1952 Vulcan contract, XA913, was the last Vulcan to leave the Manchester factory in 1957; the New Year started with the roll-out of XH475, the first of the 37 XH-serialled aircraft ordered in 1954. Powered by 13,500lb Olympus 104 engines, the XH-series aircraft were used to 'top-up' existing squadrons and to form a new one, No 617 Squadron, at Scampton on 1 May 1958.

However, only 20 aircraft from the 1954 order were eventually built as Vulcan B.1s because, although Avro had received a contract for a further eight Mk 1s on 31 March 1955 (bringing the total order to 70), the RAF had already decided that something better was needed. The main problem with the Vulcan 1 was that although the Phase 2 wing solved the buffet problem when 'g' was pulled, it added nothing to the aircraft ceiling which Boscombe found to be 'only 43,000ft' at bomb release. 'By present day standards,' con-cluded Boscombe, 'this height is too low for an unarmed bomber and must be improved as soon as possible.'

It is true that a lightly loaded Vulcan with Olympus 101 engines could reach 53,000ft by the time it was down to normal landing weight of 95,000lb, but survival of an aircraft still laden with fuel and weapons was what mattered. In the short term, up to 1,500ft could be added to the height over target by fitting more powerful Olympus 102 (12,009lb thrust) and 104 (13,500lb thrust) engines. XA889 first flew with Olympus 102s in March 1957, followed by 104s four months later, and all early Vulcans were progressively modified up to the 104 standard during overhauls.

Unfortunately the Phase 2 wing could not accept engines of much greater power without recurrence of the buffet problem when 'g' was pulled.

Such powerplants were certainly in the pipeline and as early as 1954 Bristol started work on the Olympus B.O.16, a redesigned engine with one fewer stage on both compressor spools but which, because of its great increase in mass flow, promised to start life at over 15,000lb static thrust. Bristol was also talking about a B.O.121 capable of around 20,000lb thrust in the not too distant future 'to allow the Vulcan to reach its ultimate design potentialities'; and to take advantage of the much higher operating altitudes such engines would confer, Avro developed the Phase 2C Vulcan wing. The Phase 2 wing on the B.1 had always been regarded as an interim improvement because it had been restricted to modifications forward of the main spar. When Roy Ewans took over as Avro's Chief Designer in July 1955, he and Chief Aerodynamicist Pete Sutcliffe carried on where the Phase 2 wing left off to design a Phase 2C wing with a lift coefficient of at least 0.45 at the buffet threshold at a cruising Mach number of 0.873. Consequently the span of the Phase 2C wing grew from 99ft to 111ft, and it wing area from 3,446sq ft

to 3,965sq ft, in order to provide the same wing loading as the Phase 2 wing at heavier weights. The wing outboard of the elevators was redesigned to reduce thickness/chord ratio of 8% to 4½%, the compound taper of the leading edge increased still further, the new portion was cambered and the trailing edge was also swept. Finally, to provide more aileron control on landing, the new wing was to carry four full-span elevons — two very large ones inboard and two small honeycomb-filled ones outboard — in place of the outboard ailerons and inboard elevators.

These proposed changes were submitted to the Ministry by September 1955 to be followed on 25 February 1956 by a production order for 24 Vulcan B.2s. A month later a contract was issued for the conversion of the second B.1 prototype, VX777, to act as the prototype B.2, and it was withdrawn from the B.1 development programme in August to have its wings adapted during the following year. Thus modified, VX777 re-flew on 31 August 1957 in time to appear at the Farnborough Show before starting trials to prove the new wing in flight. These trials were a great success; they proved not only that the range of the Mk 2 was some 25-30% better than the Mk 1 due

to more efficient use of the greater power — this extended Bomber Command's target coverage by 25% — but they also paved the way for the first pre-production B.2 (XH533) to reach 61,500ft on 4 March 1959. Nothing vindicated the Phase 2C wing more forcibly than the following succinct entry under Airframe Limitations in the Vulcan B.2 Aircrew Manual: 'There is no height restriction on the aircraft because of airframe limitations.'

By 1957 the Vulcan B.1 production line was in full swing but as it seemed pointless to produce more of the genre than was absolutely necessary, a decision was made to build the last 17 aircraft from the September 1954 contract and the eight from the March 1955 contract to Mk 2 standard also. This made a total of 49 Vulcan B.2s under order, to which was added a final contract for 40 more on 22 January 1958.

By the spring of that year a development aircraft had been fitted with 16,000lb Olympus B.O.16 engines, henceforward to be known as the 200 series. These new engines sat behind larger intakes, fitted in preparation for the day when the B.O.121 (300-series) powerplants would be ready,

but they could only be squeezed in by compressing the electrics. It was therefore propitious that Avro had decided to fit a less bulky constant-frequency ac electrical system into the second-generation bombers in place of the old dc equipment.

Electrical power was crucial to the Vulcan. There were 102 electrical motors and actuators in the aircraft, and power for this all-electric aeroplane came from four engine-driven 112V dc generators delivering a total output of 90,000 Watts. A dc generation system imposed no great hardships at first because many services could be powered by dc, and the limited number that could not, such as the bombing and some navigation equipment, could be supplied from ac inverters. On the other hand, dc could be stored in batteries unlike ac, and this was very important when it came to providing a back-up to vital services such as the power controls. Thus, with four generators — any one of which could supply all essential services — feeding a single busbar that supplied all needs, and which was reinforced in dire emergency by a battery bay the size of a small sofa, Avro was confident that the B.1 could cope with all contingencies. So it did until 24 October 1958 when a Vulcan from Waddington was happily transiting on a 'Lone Ranger' training exercise from Goose Bay, Labrador, to Lincoln AFB, Nebraska. Unfortunately the main power supplies failed over Dresden, some 60 miles northeast of Detroit. The engines continued to feed the generators but there was a short circuit on the main busbar so no power could get through to where it was needed. At 35,000ft this should have posed no great problem because the reserve batteries were there to provide approximately 20 minutes worth of standby power, and the captain simply asked for an emergency course to steer to Kellogg Field in Michigan. But after only three minutes the crew found to their horror that the emergency batteries were exhausted. The captain called for directions to any airport, but he was too late: with no power available, the aircraft's control

Left:
Jimmy Harrison shows off the prototype B.2, VX777, to the Farnborough crowds in 1959.

Right:
Avro flight test crew, led by Jimmy Harrison (second from right, who succeeded Roly Falk as Chief Test Pilot in January 1958) wearing partial pressure clothing designed for very high V-bomber sorties. The pressurised helmet and jerkin protected crew members in the event of cockpit pressurisation failure above 50,000ft — lack of normal pressurisation at such heights could make blood boil and the pressure jerkin prevented this by balancing the respiratory pressure inside the helmet and by exerting a mechanical pressure on the human torso.

surfaces went into the trail position and down went the delta bomber. There was just enough power left to transmit a final 'Mayday' call shortly before witnesses saw the doomed Vulcan strike a house in a residential district of Detroit at an angle of 60-70°. Only the co-pilot managed to eject, but having omitted to don his lifejacket and being the only man on No 83 Squadron who could not swim, he drowned in Lake St Clair.

The rear crew probably never even managed to get out of their seats because of the crushing 'g' forces, and the captain must have stayed to the bitter end even though, in the absence of any manual reversion, he was wasting his strength trying to put any life into dead flying controls when there was no electrical power available. Immediately after this accident to XA908, the main busbar on the Vulcan B.1 was split into two to prevent a short circuit from having such a calamitous effect again. Not that this could guarantee electrical power under all circumstances. In March 1961 XA904 crashed and, on asking the reason, an Avro executive was told that all the electrics had failed. 'Impossible,' he replied. 'Not if all the engines fail,' came the retort. 'But why should all the

engines fail?' 'Because sombody kept the Vulcan in the "stack" awaiting landing clearance for one and a half hours and it ran out of fuel!' Thereafter, an order went out that all Vulcans had to land with a minimum of 8,000lb of fuel remaining.

The introduction of a constant-frequency ac system sounds very mundane but it is impossible to over-estimate its implications for the V-bomber crews. The Detroit malfunction would never be repeated on a Vulcan B.2, not only because it carried a more reliable main ac system but also because it could carry much more effective back-up facilities. For a start, its main system was divided into two halves so that even if two alternators on one side failed, the two on the other side could carry all the loads. In the unlikely event of all four alternators failing at height, the pilots could pull a handle which lowered a Plessey ram air turbine (RAT) into the airstream below the port engine intake and this wind-driven alternator would supply the flying controls until the bomber descended to less rarefied levels, where the AEO could start the Rover gas turbine Airborne Auxiliary Power Plant, positioned outboard of No 4 engine, to take over all the essential services

until the main alternators could be brought back on line. From now on, the Mk 2 Vulcan crews would have the satisfaction of knowing that they could rely on the proverbial belt, braces and a piece of string; ac would also meet the needs of additional services such as electronic counter-measures and stand-off missiles which were then in the offing.

To save time, the Vulcan Mk 2 production line was established before the 1954 B.1 orders were completed, so the last B.1 (XH532) was delivered some seven months after the first pre-production B.2 (XH533) took to the air on 19 August 1958. Production B.2s should have followed in quick progression, but while the company was midway through the development phase of the improved bomber, Avro was suddenly asked to fit in four large electronic countermeasures (ECM) jammers and a tail-warning radar as well.

Bomber Command possessed a bevy of electronic warners and jammers during World War 2 but the demise of the Luftwaffe took much of the impetus out of the electronic warfare business. First generation Soviet early warning and control radars were such rudimentary affairs operating on

single frequencies that Vulcan B.1s could counter them with 'Window' — bundles of tinfoil strips which produced echoes equal in magnitude to those of an aircraft to confuse the air defences. However, although 'Window' dispensers remained an integral part of the Vulcan's armoury, by the mid-1950s Soviet advances in radar and missile-equipped fighters were such that height, speed and tinfoil strips alone were insufficient. Unfortunately, the addition of extra electronic counter-measures equipment to the Vulcan B.2 specification late in the day caused quite a few headaches for Avro.

Some electronic wizardry such as the flat aerial plate between the starboard Vulcan jet pipes was not too difficult to incorporate, but the tail warning radar was a different matter. Known as Red Steer after Gerry Steer of the Telecommunications Research Establishment at Malvern who developed it, it centred on a fighter radar that was taken off the shelf because it was the correct size, but Red Steer's fitment into the Vulcan along with jammers the size of dustbins demanded a new tail on every aircraft. Consequently, Avro had to design a new Vulcan tail with dimensions as large as a Gnat fighter fuselage, and Chadderton's relatively small production line could not cope with this sort of modification at the drop of a hat. Thus XH533 and a couple or so more Vulcans were produced with pointed tailcones before the first definitive B.2, XH534, appeared early in 1959.

XH534 typified the B.2 breed by embodying the new tail — which although only 34in longer than that of the B.1 was much bulkier and knobblier to accommodate all that lay therein — and the wing and electrical changes. The new ac electrical system paid dividends when ECM was incorporated because jamming demands power and each Vulcan B.2 produced enough electricity to light the streets of a small town. XH534 also carried 17,000lb thrust Olympus 201 engines set behind enlarged engine intakes, and a nosewheel leg shortened by 18in, a combination of features which embarrassed some ex-Vulcan 1 captains who forgot that not only did half as much thrust again come out but also that their jet pipes were no longer pointing at the ground. Several incidents resulted when too much power was applied on taxying, varying from the turning over of a staff car and an RAF policeman's hut to the wholescale removal of a council rubbish dump at Yeovilton.

XH534 spent its early life on development programmes, and deliveries of the Vulcan B.2 to the RAF only began on 1 July 1960 when XH558 was handed over to 'B' Flight of No 230 OCU ('A' Flight looked after B.1 crew conversion). The Vulcan B.2 soon proved itself to be a marvellous aeroplane. It was incredibly strong and resilient, yet it was also extremely manoeuvrable and could power its way up to the heavens like a bat out of hell. 'Only the British could build an aeroplane with so much power but which couldn't go supersonic,' observed an American General, but this observation overlooked the point that 204,000lb of fully laden Vulcan B.2 powered by four 17,000lb engines could knock 488,000lb of B-52H powered by eight 17,000lb engines into a cocked hat on all counts except weapon load and range. Nor did the Vulcan B.2 appear any later than the most advanced version of the B-52, for CA Release was given to the former in May 1960 whereas the first B-52H was only rolled out on 30 September 1960. Given the vastly superior numbers and resources available to Boeing

compared with Avro, Stu Davies was perfectly justified when he said proudly, 'We did not do so badly'.

The first trained crews to leave 'B' Flight of 230 OCU went to No 83 Squadron at Scampton which began exchanging B.1s for B.2s in November 1960. A new Vulcan unit, No 27 Squadron, re-formed with B.2s on 1 April 1961 and the Scampton Wing was completed five months later when No 617 Squadron also started converting from B.1s.

Consideration was given to converting all Vulcan B.1s to the B.2 standard retrospectively, but the idea was eventually rejected because each conversion would cost approximately two-thirds of the price of a new Vulcan B.2. A compromise was reached whereby the 20 B.1s from the September 1954 order and nine of the best from the original order were to be fitted with electronic counter-measures equipment in the same bulged and

Below:
Vulcan B.2s of No 83 Squadron lined up at Scampton.

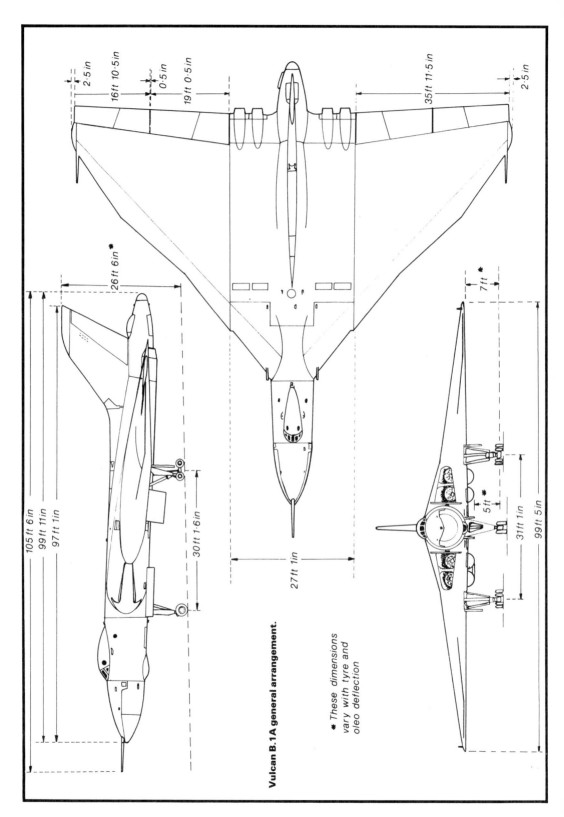

2·5 in

16ft 10·5in

0·5 in

19ft 0·5 in

35ft 11·5 in

2·5 in

26 ft 6in *

7 ft *

105 ft 6 in

99 ft 11 in

97 ft 1in

30 ft 1·6 in

27 ft 1in

5 ft *

31 ft 1in

99 ft 5 in

Vulcan B.1A general arrangement.

* These dimensions
vary with tyre and
oleo deflection

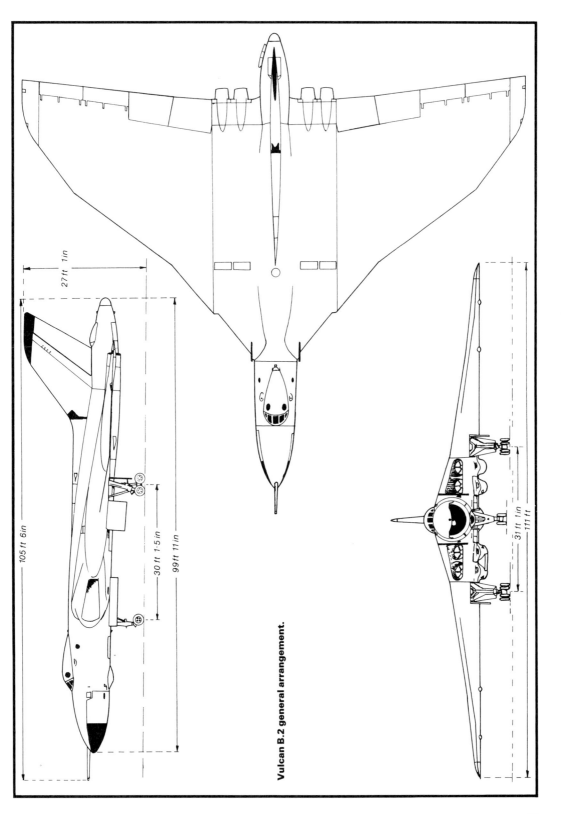

Vulcan B.2 general arrangement.

27ft 1in

105 ft 6in

30 ft 1·5 in

99ft 11in

31ft 1in

111 ft

extended rear fuselage as the B.2, plus the addition of the flat aerial plate between the starboard jet pipes. The modified B.1s were also given a turbine-driven alternator to provide the necessary ac power. The conversion programme was undertaken by Armstrong-Whitworth at Bitteswell, a Hawker Siddeley facility that later carried out many of the Vulcan major servicings with great distinction. As B.2s arrived in service, B.1s were individually withdrawn from the front-line to be converted to what became known as Vulcan B.1As, beginning with the arrival on No 617 Squadron of XH500 on 29 September 1959 and finishing with the return of XH503 to Waddington on 6 March 1963.

By this time there had been much shuffling of squadrons and aircraft to ensure that all Vulcan B.1As were concentrated on three squadrons at Waddington. The first of these was No 44 (Rhodesia) Squadron, re-forming on 10 August 1960 by the simple expedient of taking over No 83 Squadron's eight B.1s and personnel, and it received its first B.1A in January 1961. In June 1961 No 44 Squadron was joined by No 101 Squadron, which moved its aircraft over to Waddington from Finningley while No 230 OCU moved in the opposite direction. Finally, No 50 Squadron became the last B.1 and B.1A unit, re-forming on 1 August 1961 with aircraft that had come from No 617 Squadron.

Once the last B.1A had emerged from Bitteswell, the RAF's remaining B.1s were withdrawn from front-line service to see out their days on the OCU and Bomber Command Development Unit at Finningley. The B.1s had outlived their operational usefulness once enough B.2s rolled off the production line to equip Nos 9,

12 and 35 Squadrons, which formed at Coningsby on 1 March, 1 July and 1 November 1962 respectively. The Vulcan B.2 force was now complete.

The Coningsby Wing moved to Cottesmore in November 1964 where the last Vulcan B.2 (XM657) was delivered to No 35 Squadron on 14 January 1965. A year later, the Waddington Wing began to re-equip with the more powerful variant in place of its B.1As. No 50 Squadron converted first, and Nos 44 and 101 Squadrons followed suit over the next two years, the last receiving its aircraft from Cottesmore when No 12 Squadron disbanded on 31 December 1967. The B.1As, and B.1s from the OCU, were progressively moved to the Maintenance Unit at St Athan between 11 March 1966 and 10 January 1968, from whence they were either scrapped or dispersed to various training units to act as instructional airframes.

Two Vulcan prototypes, 45 B.1s (of which 29 were converted to B.1As) and 89 B.2s were produced in all, and they were all first rate aeroplanes, which was just as well considering that a Vulcan B.2 in 1961 cost more than eight Lincolns in 1946. On the other hand, the nuclear weapon nestling inside each of these 136 Vulcan bomb bays was 500,000 times more powerful than the conventional bomb of World War 2 according to the 1961 Defence White Paper, and this leads to the second part of the Vulcan story — its weapons and its operational history.

Below:
New salutes old. A Vulcan B.2 of No 617 Squadron overflies the Lancaster gate guardian at Scampton on the 20th Anniversary of the Dams Raid.

8
Flying the Tin Triangle

To understand what it was like to fly the Vulcan, it is worth following a training mission through from start to finish. The crew of five would meet together some three hours before take-off in the Operations building where the first hour would be spent preparing charts, checking weather and diversion airfields, booking bombing ranges, calculating take-off performance and so on, culminating in a full and comprehensive crew briefing. The next hour would be spent devouring a high protein pre-flight meal and changing into flying clothing, followed by a ride in a crew coach out to one of the aircraft pans which might be several miles away across the airfield. There the Crew Chief would brief on any minor problems or recent rectification work on the aircraft; the captain would sign for his charge on the Form 700 and then walk round the aircraft to check some 70 different points externally.

The AEO boarded the bomber first to check that all the systems were safe and then the rest of the crew, complete with bags and rations, would climb the ladder and strap in. Rear crew members could just about stand up behind their seats, though no more than one at a time if the two jump seats by the door well were occupied; once the pilots had ascended the central cabin ladder to the flight deck, they were virtually immobilised in their ejection seats for perhaps the next six hours.

All internal aircraft checks from the 'after strapping-in checks' to the 'shut down checks' were carried out on a challenge and response basis, with the AEO reading out each check from his Flight Reference Cards and the appropriate crew member reponding with the correct action.

Although both pilots had a reasonable view forward and sideways, there was little to be seen downwards or behind, and as the pilots could not even see the wing tips, the Crew Chief acted as their external eyes and ears on his intercom lead. A ground electrical power unit fed the various systems while they were being checked so as not to drain the batteries, and after about half an hour the crew was ready to start engines. Inside the cabin there was little sensation of an Olympus engine bursting into life; there was no coughing and spluttering as in the piston-engined days and no shaking of the aircraft structure, just a whine

increasing in intensity as the rpm wound up. Up on the flight deck a host of gauge needles rose from the dead, for as one ignition cycle had run its course another would be started. When all four engines were turning the external electrics would be disconnected, the remaining systems checked, taxi-clearance obtained from the Tower, and the Crew Chief bade a fond farewell. He in turn would proffer best wishes for a successful trip, disconnect his intercom lead, and the first pilot would release the parking brake and edge the heavy bomber out on to the taxiway.

The pre-take-off checks would be carried out at the marshalling point followed by clearance to enter the runway for a brake check against 80% power. The noise inside the bomber was muted but the fettered thrust forced the front suspension down and down until there was a positive forward slope to the aeroplane. If everything looked and felt good, the brakes would be released and the nose would rise as the four stubby throttles were moved fully forward in a firm, steady application of full power.

A screech of noise would reverberate around the airfield as the Olympus engines developed full power and the Vulcan surged forward. First pilots and co-pilots usually took it in turns to take-off, so the flying pilot would hold the control column forward in one hand and the throttles in the other while the crew monitored the three air speed indicators, temperature, pressure and rpm gauges, and fire warning lights. Sitting 18ft off the ground, the flying pilot felt he was driving an 80-ton three-wheeled bus up a motorway whilst steering with his feet, and as the Nav Plotter counted out the speed in tens of knots — about once every second until he called 'Rotate' — the pilot merely had to release the forward pressure on the stick until a slight backward pressure brought the main wheels off. Immediately afterwards the brakes were applied hard, the undercarriage retracted, and then the nose was raised to keep below undercarriage limiting speed until the three red lights went out.

Then the bomber was trimmed into a steady climb to height. Even with a full load, a 300-series Vulcan B.2 could get airborne in 3,500ft of runway, and in a 300kt operational climb be

Above:
General view of the Vulcan cockpit.

1. **Nosewheel steering engage button.**
2. **Elevator and aileron feel relief switch.**
3. **Aileron and elevator trim switch.**
4. **Press-to-transmit switch.**
5. **TFR head-up display.**
6. **Tail clearance warning lights.**
7. **E2B compass.**
8. **RAT release handle.**
9. **Engine fire warning lights and extinguisher buttons (four).**
10. **E2B compass.**
11. **TFR head-up display.**
12. **Aileron and elevator trim switch.**
13. **Press-to-transmit switch.**
14. **Elevator and aileron feel relief switch.**
15. **Undercarriage emergency lowering control.**
16. **Airbrakes selector switch.**
17. **Pilot's bomb release control.**
18. **Brakes toe buttons (four).**
Each pilot had a fighter-type control column but there was only one set of throttles directly above the airbrake selector switch. The fuel system controls were positioned on the retractable console at bottom centre. *Crown Copyright*

through 5,000ft a minute later. The beast *really* went up and the same engines that accelerated over 80 tons of fuel and metal to 180mph from a

standing start in 23 seconds also ensured that it levelled out above 40,000ft barely 10 minutes after the wheels left the ground. From then on, the pilot set 86% rpm and flew at 0.84 Mach — as fuel was used and the aircraft got lighter, it could then cruise-climb gently upwards towards 50,000ft.

The best adjective to describe the Vulcan flight deck was 'cosy' — every available panel in the front or back was full of dials or switches — and it was compact enough to enable the first pilot to reach every control of any consequence apart from the cabin conditioning and pressurisation switches on the starboard side. Much of this compactness was due to the short control column, a handgrip projecting from the instrument panel and offering no leg obstruction during ejection. Once they grew accustomed to this control column, Vulcan pilots liked it and it certainly was in keeping with the fighter-like handling qualities of the bomber.

The eight movable elevons on the rear edge of the Vulcan B.2 wing, four each side of the fuselage, acted as elevators or ailerons depending on the manoeuvre. In a straight climb all operated as elevators, and in a level turn all became ailerons, but in climbing turns the inboard two on each side acted as elevators and the smaller outboard pair as ailerons. These control surfaces were not directly connected to the stick but were

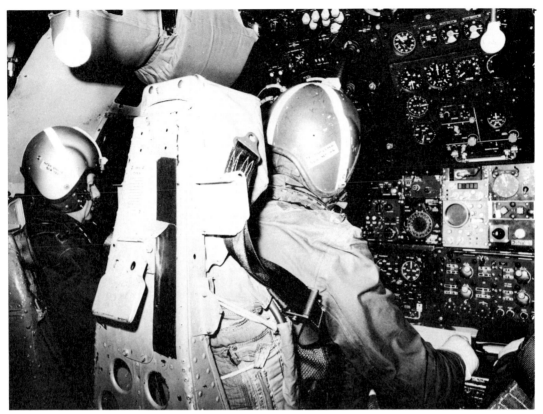

Above:
Nav Radar (left) and Nav Plotter stations at the rear of the Vulcan cabin. The AEO's position is off-picture to the right. This darkened portion of the Vulcan was likened to 'a coalmine with switches'.

power-operated: this removed all sense of feel from the controls so springs imparted artificial feel which increased in proportion to airspeed. At normal operating speeds the control forces were never uncomfortably heavy and at slower speeds they naturally became lighter. However, if the artificial feel failed, the controls became very light with the risk of overstressing the aeroplane; conversely, if a control unit or two failed, the controls became desperately heavy and big muscles were needed to fly a visual circuit.

Anticipation was the key to Vulcan flying. For example, if the nose was lowered suddenly at the top of climb, all eight elevons went down and acted as a huge flap across the whole trailing edge generating extra lift. To compensate, a pilot might push the stick further forward and down would go the elevons giving even more lift. The Vulcan was a gentleman's aeroplane but it also had to be handled like a lady.

It might be bright daylight on the flight deck with one pilot flying the bomber and the other 'playing tunes' on the central console to monitor fuel consumption and adjust centre of gravity; however, whatever the time of day, the rear crew outlook on life could best be described as 'sitting backwards in a broom cupboard at midnight'. They were screened from the pilots, high behind their backs, by a canvas curtain, and the small portholes were usually covered to exclude distracting daylight from the world of cathode ray tubes and coloured lights.

In the eerie complexity of the rear cabin, the Nav Plotter was refining his navigation skills as the Vulcan set off on its lengthy flight. Early Vulcans carried Gee, but such beacon-orientated navigation aids could not only be jammed but they were also of too limited range to be of much value on long-range flights to the USSR. Thus later Vulcan Plotters relied on self-contained devices known as Green Satin and the Ground Position Indicator (GPI).

Green Satin was a radar navigation aid designed for use between 250-60,000ft, utilising the Doppler principle to provide a continuous indication of the Vulcan's true groundspeed and drift. Simply stated, when electro-magnetic waves are transmitted from an aircraft towards the ground, some of the waves will be reflected back to be received

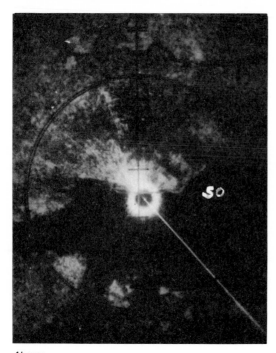

failed, the Plotter could always turn his eyes to the heavens, if not for inspiration then at least to shoot the stars by 'astro'. Two periscopic sextants could be fitted into the Vulcan roof, each scanning 180° on opposite sides of the cabin, to permit simultaneous readings by Nav Radar and AEO from two different stars for precise position fixes. Astro-navigation was particularly important because it relied only upon the unjammable heavens, but like Green Satin it was not good enough on its own to position a bomb with pinpoint accuracy after a long outbound leg. The Nav Radar's main role therefore was to operate the bomber's primary fixing and weapons aiming aid — the Navigation and Bombing System (NBS).

The Vulcan NBS was the lineal descendant of the wartime H2S radar but much removed in accuracy and sophistication. The centrepiece was the H2S Mk 9A radar developed by EMI with an average accuracy of 1,250yd from 40,000ft and 400kt. The radar display took the form of a circular map, the scale being changed at the turn of a switch from 1 : 1 million, 1 :½ million or 1 : ¼ million. At 1 :1 MILL the actual area swept by the transmitted beam covered a circle of 184 miles radius or most of England from Devon to Newcastle, but to see all this in the aircraft would have necessitated a 27in diameter screen which was much too large. So a 9in diameter screen was fitted which covered a radial range of 61½ miles, the rest of the available picture being brought into view by means of 'shift'. Shift was applied by a small joystick known as the '626' — if the Nav Radar wanted to view an area of the available picture that was off the top of his screen, he just pulled the joystick towards himself and the whole picture shifted downwards. The display could also be stabilised so that the ground responses were 'frozen' and the aircraft, represented by the centre of scan rotation, then moved over the radar screen in the direction of track at a rate proportional to the groundspeed.

Information from the H2S Mk 9A was fed through a Control Unit into the Navigation and Bombing Computer (NBC) Mk 2 built by British Thompson Houston. Given the age in which it was built, the NBC was an extremely advanced, miniaturised electro-mechanical computer which continuously computed the track, groundspeed, latitude and longitude of the aircraft from what it saw on the H2S. As such it was the primary fixing aid because, like the eye, it could actually see where it was over the ground unlike the Green Satin which, despite its sophistication, could only tell the Plotter where he ought to be — and that position, thanks to the various imput and system errors that afflict even the most finely tuned devices, could be some distance removed from where the aircraft actually was after a five-hour

by the aircraft at a different frequency from that at which they were transmitted. The amount of frequency change is proportional to relative motion between the aircraft and the point of reflection on the ground, and if this point of reflection is on the aircraft's track then the amount of frequency change can be expressed in terms of groundspeed. This was the basis of the Green Satin system which transmitted two beams of short burst pulses simultaneously, one looking forward and one aft of the aircraft, and which could then be measured on return and converted to groundspeed and distance flown. At the same time the aerials were kept in constant alignment with the aircraft's track so that automatic measurement of the angle between the fore and aft axis of the bomber and the fore and aft axis of the aerials provided drift information. Data from Green Satin was fed into the GPI, an electro-mechanical computer which was one of the most intricate and wonderful pieces of kit on the Vulcan as well as one of the most expensive, which continuously displayed the aircraft's ground position in latitude and longitude on counters.

Taking inherent errors into account, the basic accuracy of the Green Satin/GPI navigation system was two miles along track, and 8-12 miles across track, in every 1,000 miles. If these wonderful aids

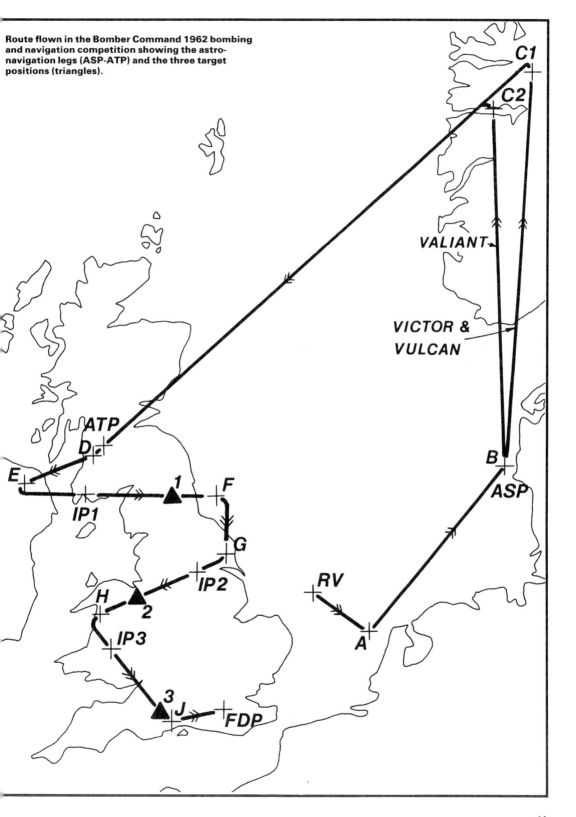

Route flown in the Bomber Command 1962 bombing and navigation competition showing the astro-navigation legs (ASP-ATP) and the three target positions (triangles).

Above:
Vulcan B.2 of No 50 Squadron in formation with four Lightnings of No 5 Squadron. *Crown Copyright*

flight. Consequently the NBS, with its ability to discriminate to within 150ft, was used to continuously update the GPI.

In addition, the NBS could also steer the aircraft and automatically release the bomb-load. One of the advantages of the H2S 9A over its predecessors lay in its electronic markers. On the ¼ MILL bombing scale these markers consisted of a variable range circle and a bearing marker whose intersection always defined the electrical centre of the radar screen, and they acted as a very accurate bomb-sight graticule.

The Nav Radar could often see his aiming point from 160 miles away and the usual procedure was to home to an easily identifiable Initial Point some 60 miles from weapon release where the navigation and bombing computers could be finally updated accurately. At 40 miles to weapon release, the Nav Radar would change over to his larger bombing scale and place the target under his aiming markers by means of his 'joystick'. If the target response was weak or impossible to identify — some targets might be underground — the bombing run could still be pressed home provided there was an identifiable reference point within four miles of the target. The co-ordinate distances of the target from the reference point could be set on 'offset'

dials and the aircraft automatically homed to the correct release point.

Once the target or 'offsets' were in, the computer could do the rest down to feeding steering information directly into the autopilot. Up front, the Pilot's Directional Indicator told the flying pilot to fly left or right to keep on the bombing track computed from the back. At 40 miles from the target, the ballistics chain of the NBS would come into operation to open the bomb doors automatically and release the weapon when the time was right. The computers calculated the forward throw of the bomb, compared this with the track range to the target, and proclaimed the difference as the distance to go. From 20 miles out, a scale in front of the first pilot counted the miles down to release point, the ballistics computer signalled the bomb-doors to open just before release, and at approximately seven miles from the high level target the bomb would be sent on its way.

As the simulated bomb left the aircraft, the

needle on the pilot's scale would drop and he would know it was time to 'rack' his bomber round to avoid overflying the detonation, close the bomb doors, and beat a retreat.

This technique held good for both high and low level Vulcan bombing, the only differences being that at low level the pilots could take over and bomb visually if they felt that the Mk 1 eyeball was more finely tuned than the NBS. Crossing the UK or North America at low level was marvellous stuff and the great triangular wing just sucked the Vulcan up over minor hills. One pilot compared the Vulcan at low level to 'a magic carpet ride — no vibration, noise shut out behind, and a steady flowing motion with climbs and descents easily accomplished. In any awkward spot the first thing to do is to put on power (plenty of it for there were tons available), then fly the aircraft to safety'. Not that such drastic action was usually necessary unless the weather clamped down; a bit of anticipation combined with the Vulcan's incredible manoeuvrability could squeeze crews through most valleys. Compared with the B-52, which needed half a county to turn at low level, the Vulcan was a dream. There were few more awe-inspiring sensations than to cleave the air and crest the ridge at 300ft in a Vulcan, especially if the sun was shining and a mighty delta shadow below personified both avenging angel and prehistoric spectre. If you dropped a bomb on the nail as well, there was no more satisfying flying in the world.

Simulated bombing runs from high or low level could be carried out anywhere, but to have some objective means of assessing accuracy crews usually operated against Radar Bomb Score Units (RBSUs). The first RBSUs were sited around London, Birmingham, Leeds and Salisbury Plain, though they moved around every few years for variety's sake, and they consisted of a radar which tracked the bomber's height, groundspeed and track as it came in by means of an automatic marker pen moving across a plotting table. The Nav Radar switched on a radio tone signal as he aimed for his bomb release point, and some indication of these aiming points from 40,000ft may be gleaned from the 1962 Bombing Competition targets which were the southwest corner of a hangar on Ouston airfield, the centre of the passenger footbridge at Hooton Park railway station near Liverpool, and the cross-roads in the small village of Enford near Salisbury respectively. The tone signal cut off and the RBSU pen jumped automatically at the point where the Nav Radar would have released his bomb; the RBSU controllers then went into their ballistics tables to work out the forward throw and to plot the theoretical point of impact. The bombing score

Below:
Fighter pilot's view of a Vulcan through the gunsight of a RAAF Mirage during an air defence exercise in Malaysia. *Crown Copyright*

was then passed back to the aircraft as a Delta Hotel (Direct Hit) or error in yards, and the crew would either go off on another bomb run or meet up with a representative from Fighter Command for a bit of mock aerial combat.

Fighter affiliation between a Vulcan and a multiplicity of interceptors over the years was always good value for both parties, and it was here that the AEO came into his own; in addition to managing the electrics and communications on board the Vulcan, he co-ordinated the defence of the bomber from missile and fighter attack.

Lacking defensive armament, the Vulcan crew had to work as a team to avoid destruction. The H2S had a modification known as Fishpool which under certain circumstances could detect fighters around and below, so the Nav Radar could sometimes see a fighter climbing. He would pass this information to the pilot, who would then try to turn away to prevent the fighter from ever finding the bomber. If this failed, the AEO would take over the running commentary as the fighter swept in behind and into the ken of his backward-looking tail warning radar. Even if the interceptor pilot got into a tail position, and the Vulcan pilot would turn into him to try and deny him this advantage, bundles of 'Window' might confuse the fighter's airborne radar for it was no easy task to keep a turning Vulcan in the firing sights. 'At its operational height,' declared the Air Ministry in 1958, 'the Vulcan can outfly and outmanoeuvre any fighter in squadron service today,' and right to the end there was no fighter that could match the great triangular wing for turning circle around 50,000ft.

But in the end, fighters could simply stand off and fire their missiles without 'mixing' it with the Vulcan, and improvements were made to the tail warning radar so that it could detect missile launch. Then the Vulcan crew really had to work for its living and trust in jamming, 'Window', infra-red decoys and 'racking round' to thwart the missiles' endeavours.

Finally it was back to base. At the top of descent, out would come the airbrakes and down would go the Vulcan at around 4,000ft/min to position for a few instrument approaches and overshoots, the pilots flying turn and turn about. In case the day ever came when they lost two adjacent engines, pilots would throttle back two on the same side and fly an asymmetric approach on the other pair. The Vulcan could maintain a reasonable rate of climb on just two engines even at maximum weight, and because the engines lay so close to the centre-line, the asymmetric problem was not great and rudder loads could be held with the feet. It was always possible to tell when a Vulcan was overshooting on asymmetric power because it sounded like a 'rutting dinosaur'.

Finally, the slide-rule calculations would show the fuel weight to be low enough for landing. If necessary, the Nav Radar could guide the bomber down from his H2S picture or the autopilot could be tied to the ILS to bring the Vulcan accurately down to 200ft before the pilot had to take over.

The lift/drag characteristics of the delta wing were such that a certain amount of 'throttle-pumping' was inevitable on the approach. Mid-drag airbrake was selected at the top of the glide slope, and the rate of descent was controlled by power adjustments and airspeed by elevators. The delta wing could be rotated to outstanding angles of attack before it stalled, and the approach attitude was at a fairly steep nose-up angle, but the rate of sink could become rather high unless checked by power.

Accurate speed keeping was crucial to a good landing. If speed over the threshold was too high, the angle of attack when the Vulcan rounded out into the landing attitude became such that sufficient lift was generated to cause the bomber to rise. The obvious reaction to this was to push the stick forward, thereby moving the elevons down such that they acted as one large flap which generated extra lift causing the aircraft to rise further. One remedy was to hold the correct attitude until speed decayed sufficiently to allow the aircraft to settle itself on the runway, but the drawback here was that the touchdown point could be dangerously far along the runway. Accurate speed-keeping and flying on the approach was therefore essential, and normal approach speeds varied between 135 and 145kt depending on weight. At light weights, accurate flying and the use of the tail brake chute could bring a Vulcan to a halt within 4,000ft of crossing the runway threshold.

When it came to landing, the Vulcan was very impressive. It could land at any weight at which it could take off, but normal maximum landing weight was 140,000lb. The great cushion of air beneath the solid triangular wing softened the landing, and even if a Vulcan landed with drift applied, the undercarriage was stong enough to pull it straight on the runway.

To ease the load on the brakes, aerodynamic braking was used. When firmly on the ground the stick was eased back and the big bird reared up on its hind legs. The effect was like pushing a barn door through the air, creating lots of drag — at 80kt the nose wheel was lowered to avoid scraping the tail and the brakes applied 'until the probe digs into the runway'.

For emergencies or when landing on short runways, the tail brake chute was always used below 145kt, and on such occasions it paid to be strapped in tightly because the drag created at 145kt was equal to the thrust from all four engines

at full chat. The chute was jettisoned before leaving the runway and the crew would taxy back to dispersal, shut down and climb out for a welcome leg-stretch after many hours in the air. They would then drive away for a debrief, shower and post-flight meal — the Vulcan, out of its element now, would revert to the loving care of its groundcrew and the protective arms of RAF policemen and their guard dogs.

If there was a Mr Vulcan in the RAF, it was Air Cdre John Pack who progressed from co-pilot on No 83 Squadron in 1957 to OC No 83 Squadron 10 years later. In between he flew Vulcan B.1s, 1As and 2s, was a display pilot for six years, and holds an endurance record for unrefuelled flight in a Vulcan, staying airborne in XL427 for 8hr 2min

on 11 June 1969 and still touching down with the minimum landing fuel of 8,000lb. Years later, another Vulcan crew beat his record by 10 minutes but they carried an extra 16,000lb of bomb-bay fuel!

What were John Pack's abiding memories of the Vulcan? Firstly, there was its take-off power and performance. During a display at Elmendorf, Alaska, John Pack got airborne in 800yd and 'whatever the fuel load, the Vulcan could always do better than anything else. Other big aircraft had to cheat with rocket assistance or water injection'. The Vulcan's power reserves certainly appealed to the rear crew.

'I was on Hastings before I joined the V-force,' recalled one AEO, 'and the Hastings had nothing like the power of a Vulcan B.2 which could take-off on two engines. When we took-off from Malta in a fully laden Hastings, we had to fly as far as Valetta before we reached safety speed, and if anything went wrong before that there was nothing you could do. After that, I never worried about the lack of an ejection seat in a Vulcan.'

The Victor had a longer range and higher ceiling on paper because of its better maximum lift coefficient and lower drag, but low wing loading was the key to the Vulcan's manifestly superior manoeuvrability and take-off performance. On light-weight trials the delta wing loading was as low as 20lb/sq ft compared with 150lb/sq ft on a fully laden Boeing B-47, and in wind-tunnel tests the Vulcan did not stall but still gave 90% of peak lift at the unbelievable inclination of 60°. In addition

Above:
Vulcan alone at twilight.

the Vulcan always managed to compensate for the Victor's theoretically higher ceiling by carrying more powerful engines. The Victor B.1 only carried 11,000lb thrust Sapphires whereas the Vulcan B.1 was successively modified with more powerful Olympus engines such that sea level static thrust was 13,500lb by 1958. 'There is no question that, if high altitude was the only requirement, the Victor was best,' admitted Stu Davies, 'For the same power it could always go higher, but it never had the same power so the Vulcan cheated.'

The Vulcan was a delight to fly. A total of around 80,000lb static thrust and an airframe dry weight not much over 100,000lb gave the Vulcan B.2 a healthy thrust/weight ratio even by today's standards. Even the lower powered B.1 left all and sundry in its wake. It could cruise at Mach 0.86 leaving the Canberra's Mach 0.72, with a third of the bomb capacity, a long way behind. There is a wonderful story of a private wager between a Vulcan crew and a steely American Sabre pilot as to who could climb the fastest out of Goose Bay. The American took-off 30 seconds before the delta, yet when he got to height he found the Vulcan B.1 already waiting for him.

No one ever exceeded the speed of sound in a Vulcan; the bomber could fly at Mach 1.01 indicated but this was only 0.98 True Mach Number because of instrument error. The only problem encountered with the excellent and reliable Olympus engine when it entered service was the 'creep' of engine speed at altitude such that it ran close to the maximum permissible jet pipe temperature. A double datum switch was therefore fitted on the Olympus 104 onwards

which allowed maximum rpm to be selected on take-off and cruising rpm when airborne to relieve the pilot of constantly adjusting throttles. It was said that the Vulcan engines and intakes were 10 years ahead of the airframe, and that the latter would have vibrated to bits had the engines been left to run at full chat.

The differences between Mk 1 and Mk 2 Vulcans were sufficient to justify a second round of in-service trials. For example, there was no autopilot on the Mk 1, and this omission made it very difficult to fly a Vulcan B.1 at height. 'Flying a Mk 1 above 50,000ft,' said 'Podge' Howard, 'is like milking a mouse,' and the addition of a Smiths Mk 10A autopilot to the Vulcan B.2 was a very welcome advance.

Apart from increased power, the other great B.2 improvement over the B.1 in John Pack's eyes came with the flying controls. Aerodynamic braking was the key to success in landing a Vulcan, and the introduction of elevons along the length of the B.2 wing trailing edge enabled a pilot to hold the delta up on its hind legs for longer after touchdown. With the introduction of elevons, the era of burnt-out brakes was left behind.

But John Pack's lasting recollection of the Vulcan, and the one he shares with virtually every other pilot over the last 25 years, was how easy it was to fly properly. 'The Vulcan,' recalled one senior officer, 'was the most marvellous aeroplane. It really didn't have any vices — you had to work at getting it into trouble.' The Vulcan could do just about anything — loop and barrel roll with a gay abandon that belied its size, turn on a sixpence at 50,000ft or 500ft, beat up an airfield at over 400kt, or drop like a stone at 115kt from 10,000ft above the Boscombe Down runway threshold and still land with concrete to spare. The Vulcan looked right and flew right, and it is one of the few aircraft which all who have serviced and flown it speak of only with affection.

9
Blue Steel and Skybolt

As it now took 10 years to design and develop a combat aircraft, the RAF began thinking about a Vulcan replacement before the first B.1 entered squadron service. Missiles were all the rage in 1954, and British strategic plans at that time centred on an intermediate-range ballistic missile called Blue Streak which was to come into service around 1965.

The only gap then remaining in the national strike force equation was strategic reconnaissance. There was no point having an offensive arm if it was wasted against unimportant targets, so the Air Staff asked industry if it could produce a very long-range, supersonic, high flying aircraft capable of survival for long periods over enemy territory while it went about its esoteric business. Known

initially as OR.330, this grew into Specification R.156T which called for an aircraft capable of cruising at not less than Mach 2.5, of reaching 60,000ft after 1,000 miles, and a range of 5,000 miles. OR.330 was to have been Britain's SR-71, the Lockheed spyplane that replaced the U-2, except that the RAF was four years ahead of the USAF in ordering such an aircraft.

Given that the Canberra had only recently joined the RAF and that the simplest V-bomber was still a year away from operational service, it is not surprising that only the manufacturers of the Valiant, Victor and Vulcan felt confident enough to tender for R.156T. Stu Davies stage-managed the battle of the brochures after the Mancunians put forward a detailed submission for their Avro 730 in May 1955, but by the time Avro had won the day and been awarded an initial contract that summer, the creator of the 730, Roy Ewans, had taken over as Chief Designer.

Ewans' initial proposal envisaged an unswept canard powered by four Armstrong Siddeley P.159 turbojets stacked in pairs behind variable geometry intakes in nacelles at the tips of an aft-mounted wing of trapezoidal form. The undercarriage consisted of a centrally mounted four-wheel bogie, a twin nosewheel unit, and

Below:
Shrouded Blue Danube on its loading trolley. British policy on the carriage of nuclear weapons in RAF aircraft was laid down by the Prime Minister on 18 March 1958 as follows: '. . . to prohibit the carrying of these weapons would limit the value of the work done in training. Dummy bombs were used so far as possible but it was necessary for air and ground crews to handle real but unarmed bombs in exercises so that they could do the job efficiently.' *Crown Copyright*

diminutive outrigger wheels rotating into the engine nacelles at normal weights up to 158,000lb; but in order to spread the runway load at maximum weights up to 220,000lb, four extra mainwheels were to be added to the central bogie which could then be jettisoned prior to under-carriage retraction.

In its original 730 submission, Avro suggested that a requirement might arise, 'for a bomber aircraft of similar performance capabilities. This bomber may carry either a ballistic bomb or, at a later stage, a powered stand-off bomb . . . If it were decided that the aircraft should be designed from the outset as a reconnaissance bomber, slight modifications in the overall design would result, but these would not affect our fundamental choice of layout, structure and engineering design'. The Air Staff liked the idea, especially as the USAF was simultaneously considering a Mach 3 bomber to complement its ballistic missiles, and in October 1955 OR.330 was amended to Spec RB.156D to incorporate a bombing capability.

As anticipated, this revision resulted in a number of changes to the Avro 730. Although the canard configuration was retained, the wing

Below:
Avro 730 layout to meet Specification RB.156D — four Armstrong Siddeley P.176 engines were to be carried in each nacelle.

trailing edge was straightened and the wing area outboard of the nacelle increased to make the wing into a delta. The span was thus extended to 65ft 7½in, the fuselage diameter grew from 7½ft to 9ft 4½in, but the overall length was reduced to 159ft. Instead of four P.159 engines, the new 730 was given eight Armstrong Siddeley P.176 turbojets which were moved inboard and housed in groups of four in rectangular section mid-span nacelles. The crew was increased to four — captain, co-pilot, navigator and AEO — and while the central main undercarriage was retained, the scheme to employ jettisonable auxiliary wheels was abandoned in favour of enlarged tandem-wheeled out-riggers which retracted into the engine nacelles. One of the more obvious changes to the 730 was the fattening of the fuselage and the incorporation of a bomb-bay, but the latter was not essential as the supersonic bomber was expected to carry a stand-off megaton-warhead missile measuring up to 50ft long.

The stand-off missile was also regarded as a means of maintaining the Vulcan's credibility until Blue Streak and the Avro 730 arrived, In the beginning, the primary warload of the Vulcan B.1 was Blue Danube, the first in a family of equally colourfully-named and wholly British-made weapons that became more compact and more powerful over the years. However, whether they were atomic or thermonuclear bombs, these lethal devices were all 'free-fall' weapons which meant

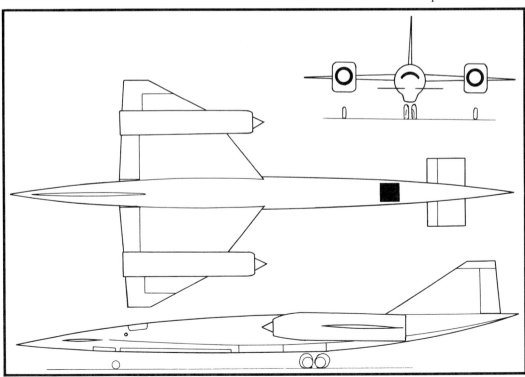

that both they and their Vulcan carriers had to approach to within a few miles of the target they were meant to attack. Unfortunately, surface-to-air missiles appeared around Moscow from 1955 onwards, and as such potent defensive systems proliferated around other Soviet targets of value, manual deposition of bombs promised to become a less and less attractive option. 'We've got to get away from this free-falling bomb business as quickly as possible,' wrote a C-in-C Bomber Command, and in March 1956 Avro's Weapons Research Division was awarded a development contract for the Blue Steel stand-off bomb to be mated with the Vulcan B.2.

Blue Steel took shape in one of the vast production hangars at Woodford where hundreds of Lancasters had once been put together. The Chief Engineer was Hugh Francis, and under his direction the Blue Steel design team carried out 23 firings with scale models before they sorted out the missile's aerodynamics. In 1958 Vulcan B.1 XA903 first showed a mock-up of the stand-off bomb to the public at Farnborough, and the following year XA903 tested the Blue Steel prototype. Vulcan B.2s XH538 and XH539 were then added to the trials programme for final Blue Steel firings over the Woomera range, culminating in Boscombe authorisation of carriage and release

of Blue Steel from an operational B.2 at heights up to 55,000ft in the winter of 1961.

Modifications 198 and 199 put a crank in the front bomb-bay spar of the Vulcan B.2 and a cut-out in the rear spar to accommodate the missile, and the bomb doors were replaced by new fairings to fit around it. The first Vulcan to have all this built in was the 26th B.2 to leave the factory, though the systems modification to carry Blue Steel, known as Modification 200, was carried out at station level. XL318 was converted first — a trolley containing all the new components would be brought out to the aircraft and a few days later it would depart with all the old bomb-bay bits on it. When modified these airframes, which were all 200-series engined aircraft, were known as Vulcan B.2As and in theory they could be converted back to conventional bombers within 30 hours; however, as more and more Blue Steel modifications and avionics changes were incorporated, this dualism became less and less practicable.

Scampton was the Vulcan Blue Steel base, and No 617 Squadron was the first to get Blue Steel. Its modified Vulcan B.2s arrived from September 1961 onwards, the station modifications were incorporated, and their first Blue Steel rounds arrived July 1962. '617' had an emergency but limited Blue Steel capability by September 1962, the missile was officially accepted into service that December, and No 617 Squadron became fully operational in February 1963, followed by No 27 and 83 Squadrons.

To understand Blue Steel operations it is best to run through the process from aircraft loading to weapon release. For a start, Blue Steel was very temperamental. Its Stentor engine for instance was fuelled by High Test Peroxide (HTP) and kerosene, and the former was lethal stuff. Unless strictly controlled and handled at all times in air-tight containers with surgical standards of cleanliness, HTP 'decomposed' of its own accord. 'Decomposition' was simply a violent eruption as the peroxide gave off oxygen at a fantastic rate, and it was for this reason that it was used to power the Stentor — at high altitudes kerosene needed oxygen to burn or it would die out like a candle in a closed box, and HTP enabled the kerosene to burn with immense heat anywhere and at any time. Thus a large water tank had to be positioned beside every Blue Steel aircraft into which a man had to dive if HTP leaked on to him, or he would burst into flames.

The Blue Steel inertial guidance system, which was subcontracted to Elliott Brothers Ltd, was integrated with the navigational equipment of the parent Vulcan; the former was so accurate that the

Above:
Blue Steel leaving its servicing and storage bay for transportation out to a Vulcan. The transporter vehicle carried the missile on movable davits in lifeboat fashion and, when it reached the Vulcan, the missile was swung outboard on its davits and transferred to a hydraulic loading trolley.

Above right:
Blue Steel on its hydraulic loading trolley which incorporated front and rear cradles for lifting the missile up to the crutch pads underneath this No 617 Squadron Vulcan. Mating Blue Steel to Vulcan was akin to fitting two sophisticated aircraft together. The missile was electrically connected to its carrier by three lanyard operated disconnect connectors each with 157 contacts, and to ensure that all these released simultaneously when the weapon fell away, the connections were not pins but just buttons that touched. Thus if something vital in these 471 electrical connections did not touch properly, the missile would not work. It took up to four hours to arm and load the missile before compatibility checks were carried out, and if anything was then found to be unserviceable, there was no question of just carrying out repairs because the missile had to go back through all the laborious chain of safety checks and warhead unloading first.

Right:
Vulcan captain, in pressure jerkin, signs for his aircraft and its white-finished operational missile in the Form 700. The range of a Blue Steel Vulcan was 1,500 miles at low level, and 2,000 miles at high level, but this was increased by the fitment of saddle-shaped bomb tanks which fitted around the missile.

missile navigated the bomber on the outbound leg while the Nav Radar periodically fed in H2S fixes to re-align the system. The inertial navigation

system suffered from a gyro wander rate of up to one degree per hour, so as near to the release point as possible the Nav Radar took a final Release Point Fix before updating the missile flight rules computer with the exact aircraft position, the direction in which it was heading, airspeed, altitude, acceleration, and attitude data, and the relative position of the target. The captain operated a switch to unfold the bottom stabilising fin, and the missile was released. For four seconds it fell freely for about 300ft to clear the aircraft, and then the Bristol Siddeley Stentor liquid-fuelled rocket motor fired; two seconds later the missile controls unlocked and it accelerated up to its pre-set height.

The Stentor was a relatively inexpensive engine and its main combustion chamber pushed out 16,000lb of thrust. This was supplemented on initial light-up by a secondary chamber which added an extra 4,000lb thrust, and the pair together were capable of sending the missile up vertically if necessary. Blue Steel's ceiling was 110,000ft, but this altitude was not conducive to range so the main combustion chamber cut out when the missile levelled out at around 70,000ft because in the rarefied air up there the secondary chamber was sufficient to sustain the speed of Mach 2.5. In this fashion the missile hurtled along under the control of the flight rules computer which calculated every change of velocity and direction from ultra-sensitive acceleration measurements made from within the missile. In simple terms, the missile knew its distance out and its distance off from the target, and it tried to fly the most direct route in between. Directional control of the missile was on the 'twist and steer'

principle by which each turn was begun by rolling with the inboard ailerons on the rear-mounted delta wing and then maintained by increasing lift on the small delta-shaped foreplanes. The inertial navigator was forever looking for a particular dive angle to the target, and when it got there after approximately four minutes on a 100-mile flight, down the missile went at between Mach 1.5 and Mach 1.8 to penetrate the defences.

Blue Steel was an excellent stand-off weapon in that it required no signals from outside to go about its business, it could not be jammed or diverted by countermeasures, and its profile could be infinitely varied from short distances at very high speed to a 200-mile range with a descent speed of Mach 0.8-0.9. On trials in Australia, using a distinctive well in the desert as an aiming point, the missile regularly landed within 100yd, and it was estimated that a Blue Steel released over London could have put several megatons-worth of H-bomb on to Manchester to within 700yds. 'Out of the last 10 shots at Woomera,' said C-in-C Bomber Command Air Marshal Sir Kenneth Cross in 1963, 'nine have been completely successful. The Blue Steel can stand comparison with any other missile system being developed anywhere in the world.'

Below:
A Blue Steel Vulcan of No 617 Squadron in flight.

Right:
Blue Steel powers off on its way while its carrier turns to beat a retreat.

Below right:
Blue Steel method of delivery.

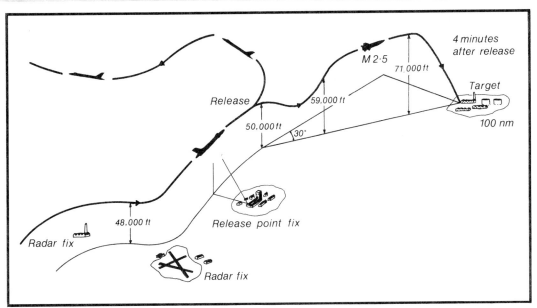

4 minutes
after release

M 2·5

71,000 ft

Target

Release

59,000 ft

50,000 ft

30°

100 nm

48,000 ft

Release point fix

Radar fix

Radar fix

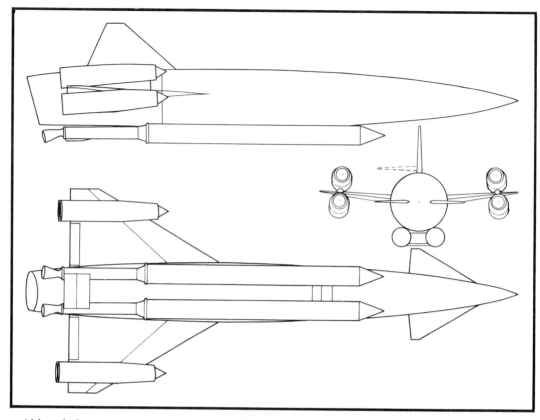

Although the greatest numerical strength of the V-force was 159 bombers in June 1964 — 50 Valiants, 39 Victors and 70 Vulcans — the greatest offensive power was achieved at the end of the same year when all the Vulcan Blue Steel squadrons were operational. 'The armed forces of the Imperialist Powers,' wrote the head of Soviet Air Defences, Marshal Savitsky, in *Red Star*,'are equipped with very formidable means of attack such as high speed, long-range bombers and stand-off weapons carrying hydrogen bombs,' and by virtue of its relatively small size and very high speed, the Soviets had nothing to counter Blue Steel throughout its working life.

In its formative years Blue Steel Mk 1 was intended as a first step in the long-term development of British stand-off weaponry that would eventually lead to an air-to-ground missile for the supersonic Avro 730. When Avro received its Instruction to Proceed for the 730 in September 1955, the firm believed that the first prototype would be flying by November 1959, but although the first test fuselage was well advanced in the Chadderton sheds by the spring of 1957, in Gilbert Whitehead's words 'it was not really working'. In fact, the Ministry had concluded that the bomber could not be brought into service 'in much under 10 years'. Given the potential of the Vulcan/Blue

Above:
Blue Steel Mk 2 with twin solid-fuel booster rockets and a main propulsion unit of four ramjets.

Above right:
Skybolt flight path. When air-launched, Skybolt would have dropped horizontally until the first stage of its solid-propellent motor fired. The missile would then have accelerated under guidance — the two stages of its motor would have burned for only about a minute in all — whereupon the nose cone would have entered a ballistic trajectory travelling at about 8,000mph and reaching a peak of around 250miles.

Right:
Douglas Skybolt with human companion — Skybolt was 38ft long and weighed 11,302lb, but as the Vulcan stood high off the ground Avro had no difficulty in fitting a missile under each wing. The delta tail fins improved flight stability and the four of reduced chord controlled the initial pull-up into the climb and rolled the missile.

Steel combination, Minister of Defence Duncan Sandys decided that the Avro 730 was a luxury that the nation did not really need until Blue Streak arrived, and certainly could not afford; consequently, the Avro 730 was cancelled in 1957.

This decision nearly broke Roy Ewans' heart, but work on an improved Blue Steel continued and by 1959 Sir Roy Dobson was talking publicly about a later mark of stand-off bomb with far greater range and penetration. It had the same fore-body as the Blue Steel Mk 1 but propulsion was provided by four Bristol Siddeley ramjets at the wing tips and twin solid fuel booster rockets on top of the main body. This was Blue Steel Mk 2, an inertially guided beast designed for Mach 3 and a range of 700-800 miles at 70,000ft, but unfortunately for Avro the company had enough on its plate just getting the Blue Steel Mk 1 into service on time. Blue Steel Mk 2 was cancelled in December 1959 after an expenditure of £825,000

— it seemed a wise decision because there was something better in the offing, and that was Skybolt.

The Douglas AGM-87A Skybolt was to be the first air-launched ballistic missile (ALBM). The penetrative qualities of 'air-breathing' missiles such as Blue Steel were much better than those of a manned bomber on its own because of a smaller radar cross-section and much faster speed, but by 1957 an even better option appeared to be the marriage of the bomber and the ballistic missile. Ground launched ballistic missiles are vulnerable

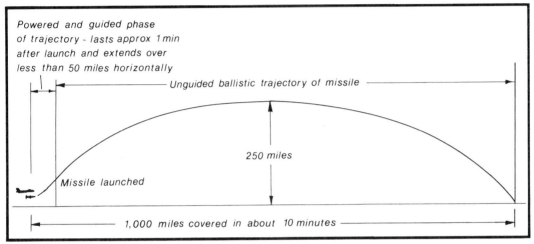

Powered and guided phase
of trajectory - lasts approx 1 min
after launch and extends over
less than 50 miles horizontally

Unguided ballistic trajectory of missile

250 miles

Missile launched

1,000 miles covered in about 10 minutes

Above:
XH537 with dummy Skybolts underneath. *BAe*

insofar as their trajectories are predictable after launch, and there was little scope for hiding their silos in the geographically diminutive British Isles. Skybolt on the other hand offered all the advantages of the ballistic missile in terms of speed, accuracy, relatively small re-entry vehicle and range of up to 1,000 miles while retaining the tactical flexibility of the aircraft. Soviet early warning stations could never keep a permanent eye on 500 million cubic miles of sky, and therefore Skybolt's direction of approach promised to be as infinitely variable as the meanderings of the aircraft that carried it. Moreover, Skybolt was seen as a very important step towards extending the mobility and flexibility of the deterrent; indeed, it could have been launched at many of its wartime targets from over the UK, and unlike the surface-launched ICBM, its Vulcan carrier could have been recalled at any time before pre-planned weapon release point. Thus, in the words of Air Minister Julian Amery, 'The V-bombers which we have on order, the Blue Steel which we have on order, and our present plans for Skybolt will carry us well into the "Seventies".'

The Douglas Aircraft Co was awarded the design study contract for Skybolt on 26 May 1959. The following February the company received an order for research and development, with Aerojet-General being made responsible for the Mach 9 two-stage solid-fuel propulsion system, General Electric for the re-entry vehicle, and the Nortronics Division of Northrop for the miniaturised stellar-monitored inertial guidance system, consisting of an astro-inertial system and star-tracker tied together by a ballistic missile computer. As the missile's flight time would be brief, the inertial system did not really need stellar monitoring, but the star-tracker (relying on a telescope looking through a circular dark area 13ft from the ALBM nose) was really only a stand-by method of determining launch position adequately. Either

way, Skybolt was thought to be sufficiently well served with guidance systems to navigate over 1,000 miles and deposit a two-megaton warhead with an accuracy measured in hundreds of feet.

The principal US carrier was to be the B-52, but in April 1960 the British Minister of Defence announced that the Blue Streak missile had been cancelled and that he was negotiating the purchase of Skybolt for Bomber Command. At that time the first ALBM was expected to enter USAF service in 1964, and be with the RAF a year later, after a high priority programme involving $400million in development costs.

Avro, as designer and builder of Blue Steel, was made associate contractor and manager for Skybolt in Britain. Coningsby and Waddington were nominated as the RAF's two Skybolt bases, and Vulcan B.2s already built or on the production line were to be converted in batches to carry a Skybolt under each wing. All new aircraft from the 40th Mk 2 onwards left the factory with internal wing strengthening and Skybolt attachment points outboard of the undercarriage plus Olympus 301 engines, each capable of 20,000lb thrust, squeezed into the wings to carry the extra weight of the ALBM. In January 1961 a No 83 Squadron aircraft visited the Douglas plant at Santa Monica, California for electrical compatability tests, and in July AEI was awarded the main UK contract for the electrical equipment to mate Skybolt to the Vulcan.

The Vulcan's bombing and navigation systems were to be used to supply basic information to the Skybolt's pre-launch computer. This computer was the only new equipment on the aircraft and it supplied position information and velocities along three axes to the missile-borne systems. As it turned out, the Vulcan and Skybolt mated 'beautifully' with no interference thanks to relatively simple circuitry, whereas the USAF had to spend $10million to achieve electrical compatibility between Skybolt and the B-52. Moreover, a Skybolt fired from a Vulcan would have gone further because the higher the release altitude, the greater the missile's range, and a Vulcan would have fired Skybolt from up to 57,000ft whereas the B-52H's ceiling was 47,000ft.

Aldermaston simultaneously set to work to design a British thermonuclear warhead to fit in the small missile nose cone, and by November XH537 was flying from Woodford on aerodynamic trials with two dummy Skybolts underneath: XH538 also carried out dummy missile release tests over the West Freugh range in Scotland beginning on 9 December 1961. During the following year Avro undertook an intensive development programme in conjunction with Douglas culminating in the dispatch of 200 RAF personnel under the command of Wg Cdr Charles Ness to Elgin AFB, Florida, to act as the British Joint Trials Force for the advanced testing of Skybolt with a Vulcan B.2.

A weapon as formidable as Skybolt only increased the likelihood of a pre-emptive strike on British bomber airfields, so in 1961 the RAF examined closely the US Strategic Air Command practice of 'Continuous Airborne Alerts' to see if it was feasible to keep Skybolt-equipped Vulcans aloft around the clock.

Vulcan Modifications 38 and 39 had been issued in the summer of 1959 to fit flight refuelling equipment to Vulcan B.1As to speed their passage overseas in the event of limited war, and No 617 Squadron began training with Valiant tankers in December 1960. Early attempts to mate probe with drogue were often exercises in frustration as Vulcan pilots had to balance their offset seating with a centrally mounted probe; what looked like a perfect approach to the drogue often turned out to be a squint-eyed miss to left or right by a matter of inches, and refuelling at night only compounded the problem. Nevertheless, over 20/21 June 1961, Sqn Ldr Mike Beavis and his No 617 Squadron crew were able to fly non-stop from Scampton to Sydney, Australia, in 20hrs 3min 17sec at an average speed of 573mph. The first airborne replenishment took place over Nicosia, the second over Karachi, and the third over Singapore, and it took approximately 12 minutes to transfer 5,000gal of fuel from each Valiant tanker. It was a pretty washed-out crew which finally emerged into the Australian sunshine.

Vulcan B.1A flight refuelling training continued with Nos 101 and 50 Squadrons such that '101' was able to dispatch three crews, led by the CO,

Below:
Skybolt Vulcan stands armed and ready for the nuclear gunbattle at high noon. Unfortunately, big though it seemed, Skybolt was only one third the size of Polaris and relatively small for a strategic missile. Its nose cone was correspondingly smaller which threw a considerable responsibility on to the engineers to produce a miniaturised guidance system of sufficient accuracy.

Wg Cdr Arthur 'Bootsie' Griffiths, on Exercise 'Walkabout' from Waddington to Perth in 18hr 7min. On his return from Gan, 'Bootsie' Griffiths intended to fly home directly with flight refuelling. As he approached the English Channel, he was told to top up once again over Waddington and carry on so that the doctors would have some means of checking crew fatigue. 'We landed eventually after 22 hours in the air,' he recounted afterwards, 'and we must have been the only Vulcan crew ever to take off south of the Equator and fly north of the Arctic Circle in the same trip.'

'Airborne alerts were not worth the candle without in-flight refuelling,' said a Bomber Command staff officer, and this was a major reason why Vulcan B.2s from the first production version, XH534, came off the Woodford line with

probes attached. Up to then a continuous presence aloft could only be maintained by rotating Vulcans every six hours; Waddington managed to mount 64 5½-hour Vulcan sorties around the clock during a 14-day exercise in 1962, but this imposed an unacceptable strain on station engineering resources.

The whole Vulcan airborne alert concept hinged on Skybolt. By 19 May 1961 a Vulcan B.2 was flying at Bristol's Patchway plant with Olympus 301 engines in the outboard nacelles, but these engines stretched the Vulcan B.2 to the limits. Avro therefore gave a special presentation to the Air Staff on 19 December 1961 of the Vulcan Phase 6. The Phase 6 was designed to weigh over 350,000lb with six Skybolts, and to cope with all this extra weight it was to have had up-rated Olympus 23 engines, an extended wing with the leading edge straightened, and an enlarged fin. There was also an extra 10ft 9in inserted in the nose so that the cabin could accommodate a crew of six seated in pairs behind each other, all with ejection seats, and a bunk at the rear for off-duty

RIGBY Non Stop from ENGLAND

"Seventeen hours fifty minutes? That makes them only seventeen hours and forty-six minutes late if somebody decides to take a crack at us . . . . . !"

Above:
In July 1963, No 101 Squadron proved it could fly from Waddington to Darwin in under 18 hours with flight refuelling. Not that the Australians were universally impressed. *The Daily News.*

Right:
Vulcan flight refuelling probe. The pneumatically-activated entrance door, which also served as an escape exit and windbreak for rear crew members, is clearly visible underneath and behind the visual bombing blister.

crew. This relatively palatial accommodation was designed to give Bomber Command a continuous airborne alert potential along the lines of SAC, and Avro postulated that if Bomber Command launched an aircraft every two hours, with some staying airborne for 12 hours with two Skybolts, some for 10 hours with four, and some for seven hours with six, 84 Skybolts could be deployed around the clock using the Vulcan B.2s already in service plus 48 Phase 6 aircraft at an annual operating cost of something over £55million. As an added inducement, Avro also offered a conventional version of the Phase 6 which could carry 38 1,000lb bombs divided between 10 in the bomb bay and 14 under each wing in large pods.

Unfortunately, all Avro's grand designs came to nought when the Americans decided to scrap Skybolt. As late as April 1962 the British Minister of Defence felt confident enough to assure Parliament that he had no evidence of any unforeseen setback even though the second-stage motor failed to ignite on the first live launch from a

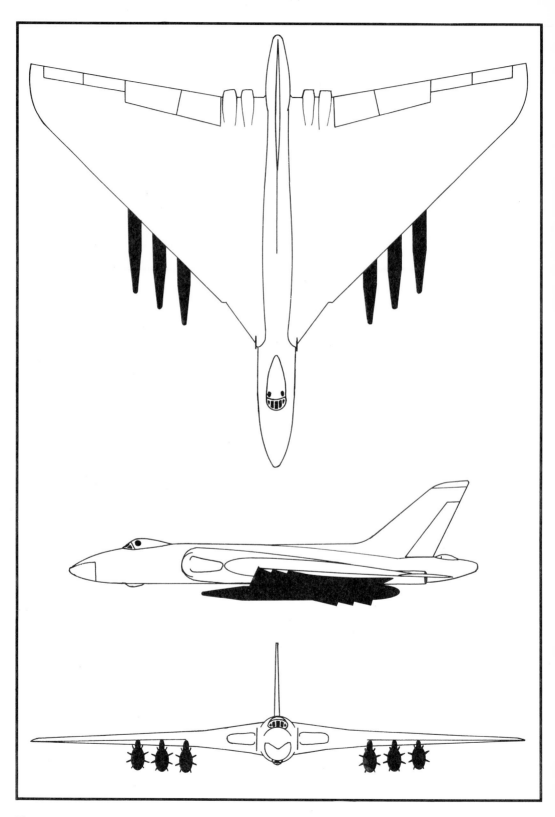

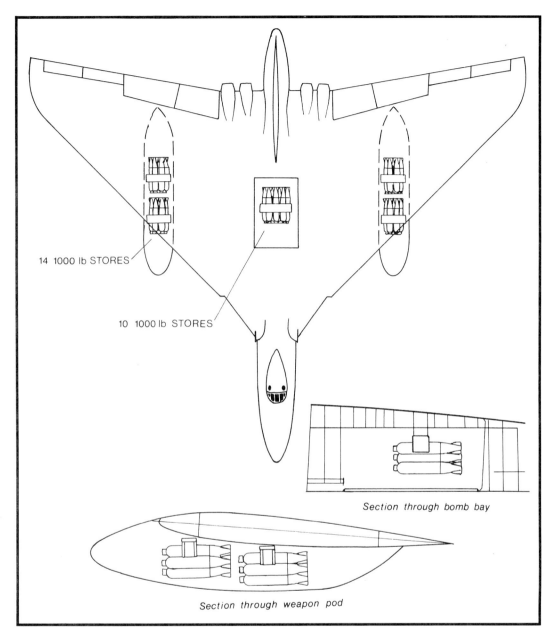

14 1000 lb STORES

10 1000 lb STORES

Section through bomb bay

Section through weapon pod

Left:
Vulcan Phase 6 with increased wing area, up-rated engines and provision for six Skybolts.

Above:
Vulcan Phase 6 in the conventional role with provision for no less than 38 1,000lb bombs.

B-52 on 19 April. There was an incorrect ignition on the first-stage on 29 June but this did not prevent agreement being reached on 10 July as to the exact number of Skybolts required by Britain.

Back in 1957 the Air Ministry had decided that 144 front-line Vulcans and Victors, each with an atom bomb, would provide a practicable deterrent, and so in 1962 it decided that 72 Vulcans, each with two Skybolts, would constitute a comparable capability.

In September, Defence Minister Thorneycroft declared that Skybolt was central to British defence policy, but that same month the third Skybolt test vehicle had to be destroyed after it veered off course, and the second stage of the fourth only burned for 15 seconds on 25

September. These setbacks probably persuaded US Secretary of Defense McNamara to cancel the whole project. The programme had already cost $500million and it promised to absorb a great deal more before it was complete, so there was no chance of Skybolt entering service at anything like its original price or within the laid-down timescale. Moreover, in comparison with alternatives such as Minuteman and Polaris, Skybolt had the lowest accuracy, reliability and weapon yield. As Polaris was already operational by the end of 1960, the US could not be blamed for cancelling a growingly expensive ALBM that it did not need, especially when the fifth 'hot' firing on 28 November plunged prematurely into the Atlantic.

It was a sad day for the RAF when Prime Minister Macmillan and President Kennedy decided to replace Skybolt with Polaris on 19 December 1962. Not only did this mean that the deterrent would eventually pass to the Royal Navy but also that the £27million expended in Vulcan Skybolt modifications plus support and training was virtually wasted. Although Vulcans would continue to practice in-flight refuelling on Far East deployments, the Vulcan airborne alert concept died that day; to rub salt into the wound, three days after President and Prime Minister met to seal the ALBM's fate, the sixth and final Skybolt was launched and it worked perfectly.

Right:
The fighter-support Vulcan, proposed in the post-Skybolt era to counter Soviet air defences by carrying three Gnat fighters underneath. The Gnats would be released to deal with trouble over enemy airspace and they were expected either to land 'in friendly territory' or return to the Vulcan to replenish their tanks from a specially installed flight refuelling drogue. The age of the 'Four Minute Warning' produced the most ambitious Vulcan proposal of all — the Vertical Take-off Vulcan. This version was to carry its weaponry under the wings for the very good reason that the whole bomb-bay was to be filled with no less than 10 B.59 engines whose ducted thrust was supposed to lift the Vulcan skywards from where it sat! Once airborne, the bomber would revert to conventional propulsion and go off on its mission. What would have happened if some of the bomb-bay engines had failed at the crucial moment does not bear thinking about.

Below:
Artist's impression of the proposed civil development of the Vulcan: the Avro Atlantic. *Avro*

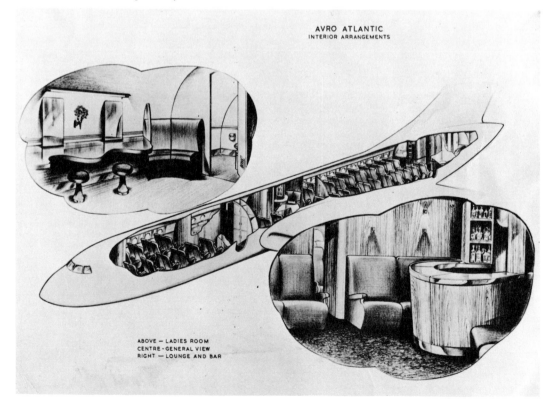

AVRO ATLANTIC
INTERIOR ARRANGEMENTS

ABOVE — LADIES ROOM
CENTRE - GENERAL VIEW
RIGHT — LOUNGE AND BAR

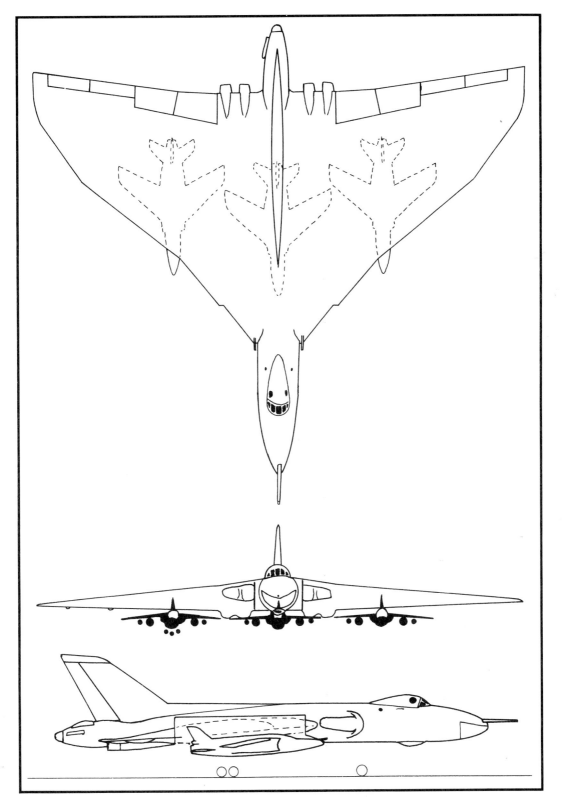

10
Bomber Operations — From Pinecastle to Port Stanley

No 1 Group of Bomber Command, with its HQ at Bawtry near Doncaster, controlled all UK-based Vulcans throughout their operational life, and the man appointed to bring the delta into service was AVM Augustus Walker, the ex-England stand-off and famous World War 2 one-armed bomber leader. 'Gus' Walker was ever a man of action and at the end of January 1957, when his Group had only two Vulcans to its name, he directed that No 230 OCU's primary commitment over and above conversion training was to prepare crews for the SAC bombing competition to be held at Pinecastle, Florida, in the autumn. It was an ambitious gamble to pit the newest V-bomber and crews against the best that the experienced USAF had to offer, and it set the tenor of Vulcan philosophy for the next three decades — never to be overawed by the opposition.

At first all went well. The two competition crews, captained by Wg Cdr Frank and Sqn Ldr Howard, took four of the six available prizes in the June RAF bombing competition, which was no mean feat given that they were up against Valiant crews who had been operating their aircraft for two years. But over in Florida it was a different story, and against hardened B-47 veterans the Vulcan crews were well and truly trounced. 'It was very much needle stuff at Pinecastle,' said one Vulcan pilot. 'We thought that the Americans were all show but they turned out to be very professional. SAC taught us a lot about how to fight and fly bombers.' Gus Walker agreed. 'We started to learn from Pinecastle,' he observed. 'We saw everything the Americans were doing and that was the great payoff we got from this involvement in competition. Like everything else, where there is competition there is challenge to improve.'

Pinecastle was only the beginning, and the Vulcan force competed regularly with SAC thereafter to spur each other on to better things.

Bomber Command crews had further opportunities to see the Americans at work when they went over to North America on training missions. The British Isles has profound limitations when it comes to navigational training because its relatively small and distinctive shape and its densely developed interior offer few challenges to an experienced crew. The snow-covered wastes of Canada on the other hand, being devoid of multitudinous distinctive features to assist the Nav Radar, are a much more realistic testing ground and consequently the old World War 2 ferry station at Goose Bay, Labrador, was expanded to act as a base for V-bomber detachments. British bombers also operated out of Offutt, Nebraska, on long-range navigation and bombing exercises and there was nothing to compare with sitting for hours out over the Atlantic or never seeing a light for a thousand miles over the 'frozen north' to bring home the importance of accurate navigation and realisation that a Vulcan cockpit could be a very lonely place indeed.

But if the Vulcan force came of age in late 1957, it would be wrong to give the impression that Bomber Command followed SAC on all counts. 'We had to face many of the problems first,' said one Air Marshal. 'We were nearer to the USSR, we were threatened before the Americans were, and therefore we had the incentive to survive much sooner than they did.' Thus, once the Soviets built up a potent Long Range Air Force and then based low-trajectory missiles in Eastern Europe, Bomber Command had to be seen to be capable of generating its Vulcans very quickly to pre-empt a surprise attack. During periods of tension therefore, groups of four Vulcans would disperse to some of the 26 Bomber Command dispersal airfields spread between Northern Scotland and Cornwall, and there they would sit at the end of the runway on specially built Operational Readiness Platforms (ORPs). As the Soviet threat to the UK grew, Vulcans had to be capable of generation and dispersal at any time of the day or night, and from February 1962 onwards at least one Vulcan plus crew from each squadron lived permanently in special caravans by the ORP on Quick Reaction Alert (QRA). Each squadron had its own method of spreading the burden, with some nominating a different crew for every 24-hour period and others keeping a crew on QRA for several days at a time to prevent the onerous duty from coming round too often. Either way, the nominated crew lived in flying suits with their whole eating, sleeping and living routine being carefully tailored so that they were never more than 15 minutes away from getting airborne in permanently fuelled, armed and checked aircraft. Cockpit readiness or engine start conditions could be ordered to shorten even this reaction time if a deteriorating international situation such as the Cuban crisis warranted it. Provision was therefore made on all Vulcan B.2s for self-contained simultaneous rapid starting of all four Olympus engines, together with quick erection of flight instruments and run-up of powered flying controls within 20 seconds. (Vulcan

Below:
Vulcan B.2 XM605 of the Waddington Wing in the snow at Goose Bay, Labrador. At this stage in the Vulcan's career, centralised station servicing had resulted in the deletion of individual squadron insignia.

B.1s had a slower but nevertheless effective 'Simstart' system of batteries outside the aircraft to start all engines.) Thus when QRA crews were summoned to action by the 'Bomber Controller' — two dozen practice alerts codenamed EDOM might be called in a typical month, half of them being up to engine start and nearly one quarter involving taxying to the take-off position — both Vulcans and crews would have been able to get airborne in well under the four minutes' warning time given by the Ballistic Missile Early Warning System.

Left:
Vulcans on the ORP at Finningley in 1977 with squadron insignia back on the tails. By this time it had been realised that centralised servicing did little for morale, and aircraft and groundcrew had once again been allocated to individual units.

Right:
A No 101 Squadron crew pelts from the Waddington Operations Block having received the order to strap in and start engines. *Crown Copyright*

Below:
A No 27 Squadron crew jumps to it from the crew coach and dash for the aircraft. Left to right: Flg Off J. Giblen (AEO), Flt Lt I. N. Wilson (Captain), Flg Off R. Howell (Co-Pilot), Flt Lt L. J. Turnbull (Nav Plotter) and Flt Lt C. A. T. Richings (Nav Radar). Notice the No 27 Squadron elephant badge behind the roundel.

By 1962 therefore, given the superb quality of the Vulcans, the megatonnage within their bomb-bays, and the fact that their crews had now come to grips with the practicalities of waging strategic nuclear warfare, Bomber Command felt confident that it could live up to its motto of 'Strike hard, strike sure'.

The proof of the pudding came in October 1961. Over the previous decade the US and Canada had, with typical American thoroughness and disdain for expense, created a superb early warning system to protect the North American approaches, enmeshed via integrated and fully automated communications to improved fighters and surface-to-air missiles. A huge exercise, known as 'Skyshield', was then laid on to test the wonderful new hardware of the North American Air Defense Command to peacetime limits, and Bomber Command was invited to take part. The RAF was more than happy to oblige, especially as it gave it the opportunity to test the new Vulcan B.2 under virtually operational conditions, and Nos 27 and 83 Squadrons were detailed to send four aircraft each. The No 83 Squadron aircraft were sent to Lossiemouth to attack from the north while the No 27 Squadron element went to Kindley AFB, Bermuda, to penetrate from the south. On 14 October both groups set off. The northerly wave began with B-47s going in at low level from 500ft upwards jamming out the ground radars. Behind them came the B-52s between 35,000ft and 42,000ft supported by B-57s, while finally at 56,000ft came the No 83 Squadron Vulcans in stream. Electronic countermeasures proved so effective that only the first Vulcan heard an F-101 Voodoo lock on, and though numerous fighters were scrambled they all concentrated on the B-52s

Above:
No 83 Squadron Vulcans in line-astern. The detachment to the opening of Embakasi airport, Kenya, was led by the Air Officer Commanding 1 Group, AVM Augustus Walker.

Below:
'Gus' Walker (far left) with his No 83 Squadron crew. The sixth member of the crew is Chief Tech Murray (far right) — the Crew Chief travelled with his bomber in the sixth seat whenever it went overseas, to the Maintenance Unit for periodic servicing, or back to Avros for modification.

Below right:
Early flag-waving — a Vulcan visits Saigon in 1958. During the campaign against communist terrorists in Malaya, small detachments of Vulcan B.1s were sent to Butterworth and Changi on Operation Profiteer at three-monthly intervals during 1959 and 1960.

so that by the time the Vulcans came through the interceptors did not have enough fuel to climb to 56,000ft for another battle and the British penetrated unscathed to land at Stephenville, Newfoundland.

The southern wave too came in 'using all jamming equipment and passive defence systems'. The No 27 Squadron aircraft penetrated on a broad front, but as they approached 50 miles from the coast, when the fighters were unleashed, the southernmost Vulcan turned and flew north behind the jamming screen provided by its compatriots. Thus, while the F-102 Delta Daggers concentrated on the three lead aircraft, the fourth Vulcan crept round to the north and sneaked through to land at Plattsburgh AFB, New York.

'Skyshield' obviously had its limitations in that the only way to see how a Vulcan would have coped against a MiG-21 was to send a MiG-21 up against it, but there was no disputing that several Vulcan B.2s at height were no sitting ducks even when the opposition knew they were coming. A few resourceful Vulcan crews had proved that they could hold their own against the strongest and most sophisticated air defence system in the world.

But if the Vulcan had replaced the battleship as the ultimate British deterrent, it also carried the mantle of the gunboat as well. The original Vulcan specification had sought an operating capability from a base anywhere in the world, and because the Vulcan was both highly visible and had the range and speed to stride the globe, the majestic delta contributed to British prestige in two ways — by impressing friends and by overawing adversaries.

In the cause of friendship, No 83 Squadron put its total aircraft complement into the air to provide the first ever three-Vulcan formation to salute the Queen's visit to Jamestown, Virginia, on 16 October 1957. The following March, the trio flew out to Kenya to celebrate the opening of Embakasi Airport, Nairobi, but equally they proved a point to the thousands of watching Mau Mau who helped to build it.

The RAF had a long tradition of sending bombers overseas to 'show the flag', and a Vulcan roaring over a jungle clearing with bomb doors open demonstrated vividly that Britian was still a world power. Thus, in tandem with its primary nuclear role, the Vulcan force always retained a secondary conventional 'iron bomb' capability. Although one Avro design proposal suggested fitting 24 540lb bombs on tandem pylons under Vulcan wings, the standard Vulcan bomb-bay sufficed with its 21 1,000lb bombs. Just as the Vulcan stood high enough off the ground to enable servicing to be undertaken conveniently via underside panels, so Avro devised new equipment to enable aircraft to be bombed-up quickly even in rough airfield conditions. The iron bombs were loaded in groups of four or seven on to septuple carriers before being brought out to the aircraft. These bombs could be released individually, in groups or all together via the '90-Way' Bomb Control installation which, as its name implied, allowed crews to drop weapons in a variety of combinations.

Given that the Mk 2 V-bombers could least be spared from deterrent duties, in the early 1960s the Vulcan B.1/1As at Waddington were primarily responsible for dealing with conventional trouble in the Middle East while their Victor cousins looked after the Far East. However, the Victor 1 bombers were due to leave service in 1964 just as

Indonesia started putting pressure on a newly-independent Malaysia, and although they were retained until the immediate crisis was over, the Vulcans were scheduled to fill the breach.

The Malaysian Confrontation reached its climax in autumn 1964. For some time the Indonesians had been engaged in sporadic guerilla activity in Borneo combined with periodic military aircraft incursions into Malaysian airspace, but in August and early September the Indonesians tightened the screw by launching sea-borne raids against peninsular Malaysia.

Faced with these increasingly bold and aggressive moves — on 2 September an Indonesian Hercules dropped 96 paratroopers near Labis — the British decided to despatch reinforcements. The situation was complicated by the fact that the carrier, HMS *Victorious*, was due to return to

Singapore from a visit to Western Australia, and it was rumoured that the Indonesians might find a pretext to deny the carrier and her five escorts the right of 'innocent passage' through the narrow Sunda Strait.

As tension mounted, Canberra bombers were brought up from Germany and Cyprus together with four 12 Sqn Vulcan B.2s. Each Vulcan carried 21 1,000lb bombs out from the UK and sat at Gan; on 18 September the 'Victorious' task group transited the wider Lombok Strait, tension eased, and the Vulcans were sent home having demonstrated once again the flexibility of air power.

The crews of Nos 9, 12 and 35 Squadrons had taken over the Far East reinforcement responsibility by the time they moved into Cottesmore on 7 November 1964, and as part of the conventional work-up No 35 Squadron was tasked with a 'no-notice' exercise codenamed 'Spherical' in April 1965. At 14.00hrs on 26 April, the C-in-C Far East requested Vulcan reinforcements and, after a short interval to simulate political release and overflight clearances, the executive order was given by HQ Bomber Command at midnight. The first of eight Vulcans, flown by OC No 35 Squadron, Wg Cdr David Craig, got airborne exactly as planned at 45 minutes past midnight after simulated bombing-up. The Squadron Commander's Vulcan reached Gan by way of El Adem and Bahrain in an elapsed time of 26 hours, and the complete force of eight Vulcans arrived in Gan in 32 hours; all crews could have continued to their targets after a further quick turn-round within 48 hours of C-in-C Far East's request. In the event, four aircraft were deployed forward to Butterworth and Tengah, from whence they could have operated if required within 60 hours of leaving the UK. If airborne refuelling had been available, the reaction time would have been halved, but even so it was a pretty impressive achievement from a standing start and its implications would not have been lost on any potential adversaries in the area.

Each Cottesmore unit detached four aircraft to the Far East for approximately 3½ months at a time; this deployment, known as the Matterhorn Rotation, continued until Confrontation ended in August 1966. 'Matterhorn' made a dent in the strategic nuclear capability back home but Far East deployments did provide some of the few opportunities for the Vulcan B.2 to be used at the altitudes for which it was designed. The Australian Air Force was always ready to provide good opposition whenever a Vulcan came within reach, and as John Pack recalled, 'they were always boasting about their Sabres. So one day we set out from Sydney, flew towards New Zealand in a cruise climb, and then turned back. By this time I was at 63,500ft with only 15kt separating me from compressibility and the stall. The Vulcan was very difficult to fly at that height — and Tommy Thompson was even higher at 64,500ft — but it was wonderful to see the Sabres wallowing about 20,000ft below without a hope in hell of reaching us.' Throughout Confrontation, detached Vulcans prepared to take on the Indonesian air defences by carrying out practice stream attacks against Darwin from over 60,000ft.

But if operations at high level were still tenable in the Far East, they had ceased to be so back in Europe. The demise of Skybolt killed the plan to retrofit 20,000lb thrust Olympus 301 engines into all the 200-series Vulcan B.2s because, although the more powerful engines conferred an improvement in ceiling, the striving after height was no longer sufficient in itself. On 1 May 1960 Gary Powers' U-2 reconnaissance aircraft had been shot down by a Soviet surface-to-air missile at a height 'above 68,000ft', and high level Vulcan operations would cease to be feasible once such missiles, together with new all-weather interceptors, mushroomed out across the USSR.

The problem in 1963 was that for nearly three years all Bomber Command's plans had rested on Skybolt. There had been a proposal to fit extra ram air turbines to the Skybolt Vulcans to power more jammers, together with a new and comprehensive jammer that could cope with a variety of radar beam widths, but the Treasury refused to fund such penetration aids for a Skybolt force that was never supposed to penetrate enemy defences. After the Skybolt hiatus, Avro came up with a variety of improved Blue Steel Mk 1s, but all these stretched versions, like the proposal to buy more Blue Steels for the whole Vulcan force, were rejected as poor value for money. The RAF even considered resurrecting Blue Steel Mk 2, but it could not be ready in time given that Vulcans were only supposed to remain in service for five or six more years until Polaris entered service.

The quickest and cheapest method of keeping the deterrent credible was to disperse the bomber force even further, including the use of overseas bases, so that it could attack from more directions, and to send the Vulcans in at low level beneath the cover of all the new Soviet radars, missiles and aircraft.

A special British nuclear H-bomb designed for low level release had been ordered for the Buccaneer and TSR.2, and the 1963 Defence White Paper reported that this lay-down weapon of megaton yield 'can be adapted speedily and cheaply to give a strategic nuclear punch'. After a series of low level trials over the Libyan desert, the Vulcan B.1As began low level crew training in 1963 followed by the B.2s at the beginning of 1964. Navigation and bombing equipment in the aircraft was not unduly degraded by low level operations, and pilots could now map-read and pass accurate

Above:
Moment of release for 21 1,000lb iron bombs. Visual bombing was not very practical over the cloud covered terrain of Western Europe, but it was a much more viable proposition in the Middle and Far East where the skies were clearer. The Nav Radar directed the target run-in from his H2S, so the bombs were dropped by the Nav Plotter lying prone at the visual bombing station.

Above right:
A Vulcan leads RAAF Mirages over Sydney Harbour Bridge.

Right:
Hydrogen bomb under wraps and securely guarded at Waddington in 1965. Until a specially developed nuclear weapon for low level use arrived in service, Vulcan crews had to fly pop-up manoeuvres prior to release to practise avoiding the effects of a nuclear explosion. *Telegraph Magazine*

visual fixes back to the navigators, so crews were cleared down to 1,000ft initially and then to lower levels when they became proficient.

This change in tactics swung the odds back in favour of the Vulcan force because there was no way that Soviet air defences could cope with a

Above:
Low-level view of Canadian snow-covered lakes from a Vulcan cockpit. The blur on top of the centre coaming is the release handle for the emergency ram air turbine.

Below:
Representatives of the whole V-bomber family — a Vulcan B.1A, Valiant and Victor — display their new low-level camouflage scheme at Goose Bay in 1964. Once the V-force went low level, North American airspace offered a variety of training opportunities denied to big bombers over the geographically confined and heavily populated UK.

Bottom:
Blue Steel Vulcan XM572 in its low-level colours.

co-ordinated low-level penetration from anywhere between the North Cape and the Black Sea. To conserve fuel, Vulcans would have transitted at height to a point just outside the forward extent of Soviet warning radar cover where they would have descended. Once below 1,000ft they would have been shielded by the earth's curvature from radar detection and would have penetrated the vast Soviet coastline unopposed. No Soviet fighter of the time had an airborne radar that could look downwards and pick out a bomber among the ground returns below 5,000ft, so the opposing fighter pilot would have had to rely on the Mk 1 eyeball. Unfortunately this would have been of little use at night, and even in daylight the amount of low cloud present on an average day in Western Europe would have done nothing to assist the defences. In fact their problem of finding the V-force was compounded still further when the upper surfaces of all Vulcans were camouflaged in green and grey early in 1964.

Low level equipment trials were carried out by the Bomber Command Development Unit (BCDU) at Finningley. Boscombe Down was responsible for aircraft trials but the BCDU, with its motto 'Improve', tested all new bomber equipments and perfected the tactics best suited to

Above:
Vulcan low-level penetration profile.

their use. At this stage the BCDU had a Vulcan B.1A and a B.2, and a typical task involved the testing of an electronic jammer in association with the GPO to ensure that it did not interfere with the national telecommunications network. When the Vulcans went low-level, the BCDU perfected a pilot's visual bombsight to back up the radar. This sight was a piece of etched perspex, a rather rudimentary aid which illustrated the hasty and makeshift nature of going low-level. However, the fact that only such relatively minor modifications were needed to adapt the Vulcan force to its new regime said a great deal for the versatility of both aircraft and equipment.

The Blue Steel squadrons were also forced down to low level as Soviet SAM sites increased in number such that standing off at high level was no longer to any avail. After low-level firings at Woomera had proved to be '100 per cent effective', the Blue Steel force became operational at low level in 1964. Modifications to individual missiles were not extensive, the main difference from before being that the two combustion chambers now fired together. The release range however was reduced to 25-50 miles at low level instead of 200 miles up high, and when it was at release point the bomber had to climb sufficiently to give the missile room to fall away before it fired. The Blue Steel then zoomed to 17,000ft, at which point the Stentor cut out, leaving the missile to hurtle down and detonate within a theoretical accuracy of 300yd.

When Air Marshal Sir John Grandy, C-in-C Bomber Command from September 1963, held a press conference at Wittering to show the Mk 2 V-bombers to the world, he said that there were six factors on which the penetration of enemy airspace depended; aircraft performance, evasive routeing (with or without air refuelling), high and low level capability, electronic countermeasures, the success of earlier strikes on enemy defences, and stand-off weapons. The Vulcans had the lot after 1964, and after showing the Press a map of the USSR with a line extending 1,350 miles from Murmansk in the north to Odessa in the south, Sir John said that the V-force could penetrate that line anywhere or fly round the ends. With a maximum high level speed of Mach 0.93 and a low level dash speed in excess of 400kt, the Vulcan B.2 underlined Sir John's conclusion that, 'penetration by aircraft of Bomber Command of areas covered by the most modern and sophisticated air-defence systems could not be successfully prevented'. For the rest of the decade the Vulcan was unstoppable.

In fact the Vulcan was so good that in 1968 it was decided to keep approximately 60 of the delta bombers in service after the introduction of Polaris. To compensate for the cancellation of TSR.2, the Ministry of Defence had decided to replace the tactical Canberra with variable-geometry aircraft built in co-operation with France, but as these aircraft would not be ready until the mid-1970s, the intervening period was to be filled by the purchase of 50 F-111Ks from the US. Unfortunately, the F-111K plan then went the way of TSR.2, so the Vulcans had to be kept in service until 1975 to fill the tactical bomber gap between the demise of the Canberra and the arrival of something better. The fact that the RAF eventually kept the Vulcan soldiering on until the introduction of Tornado in 1982, and moreover in a low level role diametrically opposed to that for which it had been conceived, says everything about the brilliance of the original Vulcan design.

It was only the massive strength of the Vulcan airframe that made this extension of service possible. Ideally, it would have been preferable to produce a new Vulcan for low level operations

with about one-third the wing span and improved systems, but this would have been to reduce the chances of detection and increase speed rather than to enhance fatigue life because the Vulcan B.2 was built to last. In the quest for simplicity and speed of construction, Avro built the Vulcan structure around two mass-spar booms with mechanical joints because the Firm had perfected this technique on the Lincoln and Shackleton. Fortunately both the RAF and the South African Air Force had bought the Mk 3 Shackleton, and the strain imposed on the section spars by low-level flight from the North Sea to the Tropics occurred in plenty of time for Avro to become well versed in the fatigue implications of mass-spar booms by the time the Vulcan went low-level.

Avro placed the 60th production Vulcan B.2 airframe, which had never flown, into a test rig where powerful hydraulic jacks simulated the gusts and manoeuvre loadings of a four-hour flight in about eight minutes. In this fashion, the fatigue specimen accumulated simulated flying hours far in excess of those clocked up by operational aircraft, so when cracks started to appear on the rig, remedial action could be taken on the fleet in good time.

Skybolt wing strengthening modifications to the 300-series-engined Vulcan B.2s proved a boon in

Below:
The top surfaces of this Vulcan B.2 are completely camouflaged to minimise detection by a fighter pilot looking downwards — note how it blends in with the scenery at low level. The undersurfaces however are painted white to minimise detectability at height from a fighter climbing upwards. Wags said that if the Vulcan had to penetrate at low level over snow, it could always fly inverted.

the low-level role, and as the years went by enough reinforcing iron plates were bolted into Vulcan wings to add up to 10,000lb to the basic aircraft weight. But it all paid dividends in the end. Although the original Vulcan specification called for a life of 3,900 flying hours in the *high-level* role, Avro estimated that its creation was sturdy enough to survive for 5,900 hours. This the company termed 100% fatigue life, or 100 Fatigue Indices (FI), but by the end the Vulcan was cleared to 320 FI in the *low-level* role, or 484% of the original requirement. Given that the Victor B.2 cracked up under the strain of low-level operations as early as

Left:
Terrain Following Radar (TFR) cylinder installed just below the refuelling probe in the radome. The aircraft belonged to No 35 Squadron and this photograph was taken during the last major Vulcan deployment to Luqa, Malta, in 1978.

Below:
TFR mode of operation. The radar emitted a pencil beam ahead and below the aircraft using a slant range of 9,000ft as the measuring parameter. If the ground ahead of the Vulcan rose, the radar return would give a slant range of less than 9,000ft and the TFR would compute a pitch-up signal to the pilot. Conversely, if the ground fell away the slant range would exceed 9,000ft and the TFR would produce a dive demand.

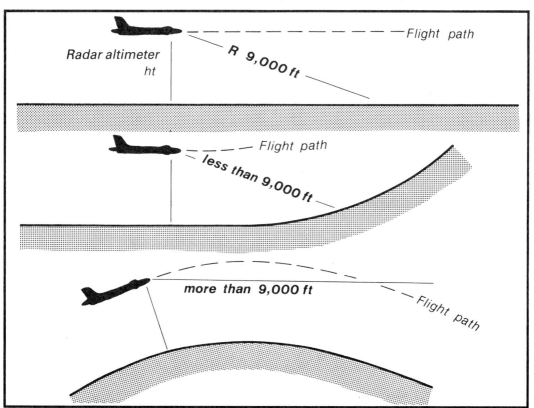

climb or dive signals displayed on his instruments. Further improvements were also made to Vulcan navigation and electronic countermeasures equipment over succeeding years.

Once the Vulcan went low-level however, the problem of aircraft accidents and abandonments became more acute. While the Vulcan flew high level operations, it was felt that there would be sufficient time for the rear crew to make a free-fall exit from the floor hatch. Thus only the pilots had ejection seats specially designed by Martin-Baker to clear the lofty Vulcan tail fin.

Martin-Baker, however, was unhappy with the overall arrangement even before the Vulcan entered service, especially as the company's design studies indicated that it would be technically feasible to fit ejection seats for all crew members. Fresh impetus was given to the question by the Vulcan accident at London Airport, followed by the Detroit disaster which proved that unless the bomber remained under control, the rear crew might find it impossible to reach the escape hatch. Boscombe certainly found this when it reported as follows on rear crew escape trials from XA892 at the end of 1958:

'Flight trials below oxygen height have indicated that, with the aircraft *under control* and in the clean configuration, fully equipped rear crew members can reach the door with up to +1¼g applied and can successfully leave the aircraft at speeds up to 350kts (the current aircraft limiting speed). . .

'However, if the aircraft is out of control and the flight path is materially different from straight and level, aircrew may find it impossible to leave their seats and reach the door. . .

'Under operational conditions the catastrophe making escape necessary may also cause loss of control and the subsequent fluctuating 'g' loads and attitude of the aircraft may make movement from the rear crew positions impossible. . . Neither pilot should eject until all rear crew members have made their escape as air blast in the cabin with the pilots' hatches jettisoned makes movement difficult. . . For these reasons it is considered that the only sure method of escape is the *ejector seat*, and the early fitment of these for rear crew members is strongly recommended.'

1969, there was no denying the robustness of the delta design. 'Ironically,' said Stu Davies, 'if the RAF had asked for a low-level bomber in the beginning, the Vulcan wouldn't have been at all like it was.'

But if the Vulcan airframe could withstand the strains and stresses of low-level flight until the mid-1980s — and Avro could have extended the aircraft's life up to the end of the century if necessary — the equipment inside the bombers had to be enhanced to maintain operational effectiveness into the 1970s. Low-level flight for instance was perfectly manageable in good daylight weather, but night or bad visibility could obscure potentially embarrassing obstructions like steep hills. It also took time to disturb 80 tons of inertia so Terrain Following Radar (TFR) was introduced to enable aircraft to contour-fly safely at low level. A number of TFRs were then under development, and Bomber Command chose one made by General Dynamics which it incorporated into the Vulcans after 1966. This TFR was mated with a radar altimeter so that all a pilot had to do was to select the height at which he wanted to fly, and the equipment would keep him separated from any obstacles so long as he religiously followed the

Consequently, in 1960 Martin-Baker was lent a Valiant aircraft by Bomber Command, into the rear crew compartment of which was fitted a specially designed rearward-facing ejection seat. Three dummy test ejections were successfully carried out from this aircraft, one at runway level, one at 200ft and 250kt, and the third at 200ft and 300kt. On 1 July 1960, W. T. Hay made a live ejection from this seat from 1,000ft at 250kt; this

completely successful ejection was witnessed by
several officers from Bomber Command and the
Ministry of Aviation and it was a clear demonstration that this type of ejection seat was entirely
feasible and that Martin-Baker was capable of
undertaking the task of modifying all Vulcans.

In fact the company was so confident of its
ability to fit ejection seats into the V-bombers that
it undertook, at its own expense, to fit three
specially designed rearward-facing ejection seats
into a Vulcan fuselage loaned by Bomber
Command. At no time did Martin-Baker seriously
consider fitting downward-firing ejection seats into
the V-bombers, as the Americans did with their
rear crew seats on the B-52, because downward-
firing seats are of little use below 800ft and
therefore 'we felt strongly that the seats would not
be effective in recovering crews in low altitude
ejections, a flight regime in which most emergencies requiring abandonment arise'. The proposed Vulcan escape arrangements therefore
began with either pilot operating a lever which
would jettison the canopy over the Plotter's head.
As the canopy left the aircraft, a cartridge would
fire releasing gases to retract all shoulder
harnesses, thereby pulling each rear crew member
into an upright position to prevent spine damage,
and to fold the rear crew table to give leg
clearance. This done, the pilots would then
operate the crew ejection control, which first fired
the Plotter in the centre; once he was clear the Nav
Radar's seat would have been pulled automatically
into the centre under the hatch and fired, followed

by the AEO in quick succession. The whole
business took less than three seconds, and as the
last seat went it removed a block in the pilots'
firing mechanism, allowing each pilot to take
independent ejection action. In all, 20 satisfactory
tests with the seats were carried out, including
airborne and sled trials up to 460kts, and they all
proved that the rear crew could clear the Vulcan
fin by 5½ft as low as ground level in straight and
level flight down to 130kt.

Yet despite Avro studies which indicated that
such modifications were feasible, the Ministry
decided that the problems to be overcome in
maintaining pressure cabin structure, re-routeing
control runs, etc, were too complex and that
aircraft just could not be spared from the front line
for the 'quite considerable' period to fit rear crew
ejection seats. Not that nothing whatsoever was
done. Swivel seats (for the Nav Radar and AEO)
and assistor cushions were fitted so that in a crisis
the rear crew could be lifted bodily to their feet by
compressed air, allowing them to fall towards the

A Vulcan B.2 of the Near East Air Force Bomber Wing off Cyprus. It was an Akrotiri based aircraft that probably suffered the most ignominious fate of any Vulcan. On returning from an air defence exercise, XJ781 crash-landed at Shiraz, Iran, on 23 May 1973 when the port undercarriage refused to lower. Although the crew survived a good landing in the circumstances, XJ781 broke its back when its sliding progress was halted by a deep storm drain. Being beyond economic repair, XJ781 was given to the Iranians and the airframe reportedly ended up being converted into beer cans.

door and out to safety. A static line attachment ensured correct parachute deployment when clear of the bomber, and a crew which practiced diligently in the escape drill trainer could get out in under 10 seconds.

Every time a Vulcan crashed, arguments raged as to the morality of giving pilots more protection than rear crews, but it has to be said that there were times when the debate was academic. For example, at 14.50hrs on 11 February 1966 the crew

of Vulcan B.2 XH536 out of Cottesmore throttled back at the end of a high level navigation stage and descended over the English Channel towards Devon. At 1,500ft the Vulcan broke clear of the main cloud base revealing the grey scud of the Bristol Channel through some patchy stratus which broke up as the aircraft approached the Welsh coast. Airbrakes came in, throttles were opened, and the low-level leg began.

Driving in fast from the coast at 15.08hrs towards the first turning point in the Vale of Neath, the Vulcan was edged up towards the overcast by rising ground. Two minutes later, Mrs Price, a housewife at Pant-y-ffordd, paused in her household chores and thought she heard a strange sound coming from the quarry at Fan Bwlch Chyth. Swathed in freezing mist 450ft directly below the trig point on the mountain, the quarry men heard nothing.

It was the Air Sea Rescue helicopter crew which first noticed the long black streak on the white shoulder of Y Gelli at first light. The harsh clamour of the rotor blades was muted by the

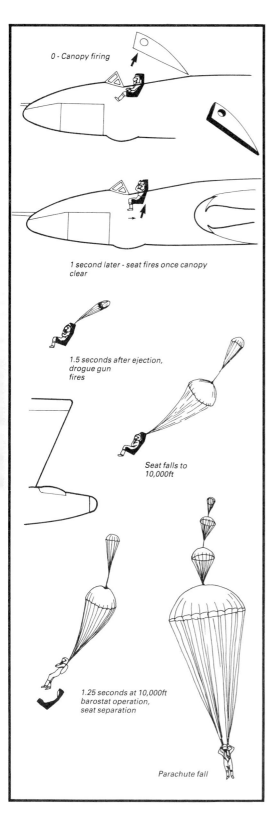

0 - Canopy firing

1 second later - seat fires once canopy clear

1.5 seconds after ejection, drogue gun fires

Seat falls to 10,000ft

1.25 seconds at 10,000ft barostat operation, seat separation

Parachute fall

silence of the mountains and the tragic sight of the half mile stretch of torn metal. To the Vulcan crew thrown from the shattered remains of their cockpit over the 1,980ft icy summit, the provision of ejection seats would have availed them nothing.

But if the Vulcan could not withstand being flown into a hill at 300kt, it was strong enough to give some crews time to get out in a crisis, as one accident report recorded:

'1. In order to climb his aircraft from low level because of deteriorating weather ahead, the captain increased power from 75% RPM to 85% on all four engines. As he raised the nose of the aircraft there was an explosion on the port side and the aircraft lurched. No 1 engine RPM ran down, the associated JPT (Jet Pipe Temperature) reading increased to the limit of the gauge, and the fire warning light illuminated. Standard fire drills were completed; the flames which the AEO had seen trailing from No 1 engine then ceased and the fire warning light went out.

'2. The captain continued to climb the aircraft on three engines. The No 2 engine JPT then started to rise and the No 2 fire warning light illuminated; the engine was shut down and fire drill carried out. The AEO checked in his periscope and could see no sign of fire. At the captain's request the AEO began reading out the emergency drills from the Flight Reference Cards when he noticed a glow in his periscope, and further inspection showed that there were flames on the undersurface of the port wing in the region of No 1 engine. No 2 engine fire warning light re-illuminated and remained on for two minutes. An intense fire was now burning.

'3. A 'Mayday' call was transmitted and the rear crew ordered to prepare to abandon the aircraft. The captain delayed the rear crew bale out until the aircraft was clear of a cloud and over open country. 10 minutes after the initial failure the rear crew baled out successfully. The captain and co-pilot remained in the aircraft in an attempt to save it by flying toward a diversion airfield. The captain started a low speed handling check but discontinued it at 185 knots when the aircraft became increasingly difficult to control. The captain decided that he and the co-pilot would have to abandon the aircraft, and after heading it towards the sea he jettisoned the canopy. The full extent of the fire could then be seen for the first time by the captain; the port wing was covered in flames and smoke. The co-pilot ejected on a visual signal from the captain who then followed.

Left:
Vulcan high level ejection sequence. Vulcan ejection seats had a ground level ejection capability at a minimum forward speed of 90kt.

'4. After the captain had ejected, the aircraft entered a spiral dive and struck the ground; it was completely destroyed on impact.'

The cause of this accident was fatigue failure at the root of the high pressure turbine blade on No 1 engine; the loose blade then jammed in the periphery of the turbine disc and rotated with it, finally causing an explosive rupture of the engine combustion chamber. The debris from this explosion damaged No 2 engine and the aircraft fuel system, leading to an uncontrollable, fuel-fed fire.

The most famous instance of turbine blade detachment occurred on 30 January 1968 when Flt Lt Pete Tait and his crew took off in Vulcan XM604 for a high level sortie from Cottesmore. On the climb out the bomb-bay temperature was found to be increasing so the captain decided to abandon the sortie and return to base to burn off fuel in the circuit down to landing weight. He flew one approach and then the co-pilot flew an ILS circuit from which he was just overshooting when Cottesmore Air Traffic warned of a contact ahead. As he could not see it, Tait took control and started to turn left away when there was an explosion followed by reverberating thumps and excessively severe vibration which made it impossible to read the instrument panel. The captain tried to level the wings but nothing happened, and as the angle of bank reached 30° to port he ordered the rear crew to abandon the aircraft. This order was acknowleged. Pete Tait continued his attempts to control the aircraft by use of trim, rudder and closing the throttles, but as all were to no avail he ordered the co-pilot to eject. After he had gone, the captain looked behind to see what had become of the rear crew but the blackout curtain was down behind him. As the controls still had no effect, and as the aircraft was now in such a steep nose-down attitude that he was hanging in his straps, the captain decided to eject. The Vulcan crashed into the yard of Cow Close farm some two miles south of Cottesmore, killing the rear crew.

The captain and co-pilot survived but the former was lucky to do so. Tait had waited so long in an effort to save his rear crew that his ejection seat should have fired him into the ground, but as his parachute vainly tried to deploy in time, his seat passed between a set of power cables 35ft above the ground and these acted as a brake on his parachute. This caused an electrical short, the captain's fall was slowed so that he landed in an upright position, and all he had to do was release himself and walk away.

After these accidents, Avro and Bristol Siddeley proposed fitting a containment shield inboard of the inner engines to protect the bomb bay and another outboard of the outer engines to protect the wing. To prove these shields engineers tried to make an Olympus fail in a disused railway tunnel near Shepton Mallet, but the engine was so resilient that it failed to rupture despite being run for long periods at full power. The only way it could be made to fail within a reasonable timescale was to disconnect the oil supply and hack-saw through the bearing gauge.

Yet despite the horrors of individual accidents, it must be said that the total loss of Vulcan B.2s from all causes remained low and represented a wastage rate not much greater than one half of 1% per year throughout the aircraft's in-service life. In flight safety terms, the write-off rate for all Vulcans was only 0.33 per 10,000 hours, a fine record for a front-line aircraft with over 25 years of operating service in a demanding role by day and night. With its great reserves of engine power and structural strength to cope with all but the most dramatic crisis, no aircraft could have served its air and groundcrews better than the Vulcan.

Thus, although responsibility for the United Kingdom's contribution to NATO's strategic deterrent forces was transferred to the Royal Navy on 30 June 1969, the Vulcans still had enough life left in them to carry on. Blue Steel on the other hand was coming to the end of its operational usefulness because of its short range, while also being expensive in manpower to maintain, and No 83 Squadron lost its missiles first when it disbanded on 29 August 1969. The Squadron's aircraft were then returned to Hawker Siddeley for removal of Blue Steel fittings and replacement of bomb-doors before returned to Scampton so that No 27 Squadron could revert completely to the free-fall role by 1 January 1970. This individual conversion of aircraft took time, which explains why No 617 Squadron only flew its last Blue Steel sortie on 21 December 1970 before completing the transition to free-fall in the New Year. From now on, Nos 27 and 617 Squadrons at Scampton, and Nos 44, 50 and 101 Squadrons at Waddington, would continue in the tactical free-fall service of NATO.

These were now the only Vulcan squadrons left in Britain because at the beginning of 1969 the Cottesmore Wing of Nos 9 and 35 Squadrons had moved out to Akrotiri in Cyprus. There they replaced four Canberra squadrons as the Near East Air Force Bomber Wing to provide CENTO with a nuclear punch as well as a powerful back-up for NATO's southern flank. Vulcans now trained on low-level routes from Calabria to Iran, and their transfer to Akrotiri dispersed the force still further since missions could now be mounted from Masirah and Malta as well as Cyprus itself.

Once Nos 9 and 35 Squadrons departed for sunnier climes, the Far East conventional re-

Top:
No 35 Squadron Vulcans scramble from their dispersal at Masirah in the Persian Gulf. Everything attached to a Vulcan on the ORP, such as the ground power unit and telescramble link, was designed to release automatically as the aircraft rolled forward on to the runway. On practice scrambles, Vulcans have been known to crush chocks left in their way to matchwood. To illustrate the speed with which Bomber Command could get off the ground, the average scramble time from engine start to four aircraft airborne was 1min 47sec at the 1960 Farnborough Show.

Above:
No 101 Squadron Vulcan over Kilimanjaro in 1960.

Above right:
Blue Steel Vulcan over Niagara Falls.

inforcement commitment was taken over by Waddington, as No 44 Squadron demonstrated in 1970 when its Vulcans deployed to Tengah as part of Exercise 'Bersatu Padu'. The standard Vulcan route to the Far East lay across France and the Mediterranean to Cyprus, to Bahrain or Masirah via Turkey and Iran, across the Indian Ocean to Gan, and thence to Singapore; if everything went well, Vulcans could double-stage with two-hour turn-rounds in between, and reach Singapore in two days. This Eastabout route was the shortest and quickest but it did involve transit over a multiplicity of nations, any one of which could close its airspace in time of tension; consequently, Vulcans also flew Westabout over North America and the Pacific which, although it took longer — about 30 flying hours — gave crews more daylight in which to operate and was more dependable politically.

Either way, crews continued to demonstrate that Britain retained a weapons system capable of mounting a formidable day and night capability within hours of arriving on the other side of the globe. In other words, Vulcans were kept in service to meet eventualities that a Polaris submarine was not in a position to fulfil effectively or flexibly, and whether they waved the big stick

Above:
Vulcan SR.2 of No 27 Squadron — the squadron crest was an elephant so all aircraft carried a picture of 'Dumbo' on the tail, courtesy of Walt Disney. The pod under the wing, which was a modified Sea Vixen drop tank attached to the Skybolt hardpoint, carried air sampling equipment. Although Avro considered the matter in depth, no underwing fuel tanks were ever fitted to a Vulcan.

Right:
A No 27 Squadron aircraft on maritime reconnaissance duty over a North Sea oil rig.

by reinforcing overseas commands during limited wars or simply impressed friends at air displays with what Americans dubbed 'the aluminium overcast', the Vulcans added an extra dimension to the deterrent. The 1969 Statement on Defence put the cost of the Vulcan medium bomber force of 1,100 servicemen and civilians at £5million annually, or one farthing in the pound of the nation's gross national product. It was a bargain.

Excluding research aircraft, there were now some 60 Vulcan B.2s left in operational service and these few remaining cards in the RAF's long-range bomber pack were henceforward shuffled at regular intervals. Thus although No 27 Squadron disbanded as a bomber unit on 29 March 1972, it re-formed at Scampton on 1 November 1973 as a maritime radar reconnaissance squadron to replace the Victor B.2(SR)s of No 543 Squadron. Back in a high level role, '27' was now employed to help counter the growing Soviet naval threat because a Nav Radar in two five-hour sorties could plot every vessel on the Norwegian Sea from his H2S screen. No 27 Squadron eventually acquired five ex-Blue Steel and four ex-free-fall bombers, and over succeeding years these Vulcans were standardised and modified with improved navigation, radar and countermeasures equipment. As No 27 Squadron's aircraft lost their TFR nose cones, had underwing pods attached, and retained their gloss paint finish, the genre became known as the Vulcan SR.2.

Shortly after the Cyprus Wing returned to Akrotiri from a CENTO air defence excercise in June 1974, Greek and Turkish emnities spilled over into war. The Vulcans were put on standby alert and flew reconnaissance missions to monitor the build-up of the Turkish invasion fleet, but although the Near East Air Force Bomber Wing tried to carry on as normal for the rest of the year, Nos 9 and 35 Squadrons were told in December that they would be re-assigned to NATO duties in the UK. No 9 Squadron returned to Waddington while '35' moved to Scampton, where they both became operational on 1 March 1975. The Vulcans then saw out their days within sight of Lincoln Cathedral divided between No 230 OCU and Nos 27, 35 and 617 Squadrons at Scampton, and Nos 9, 44, 50 and 101 Squadrons at Waddington. The only difference between the two wings was that Nos 35 and 617 Squadrons flew mainly 200-series engined aircraft and had a secondary maritime radar reconnaissance role in support of No 27 Squadron, whereas their Waddington colleagues had most of the 300-series Vulcans and retained an 'iron-bomb' capability.

Although the Vulcan never failed to impress public and politicians from Alaska to New Zealand, it retained its bite as well as its bark to the very end. Almost every year after Pinecastle, Vulcan crews took part in the SAC Bombing Competition and in 1974 as on previous occasions,

Above:
Prince Charles prepares to get airborne in a Vulcan in 1971. The captain, Flt Lt Peter Perry, is second from right.

Below:
Flt Lt Perry (front, right) holding the Mathis Trophy after the 1974 SAC bombing competition at Barksdale, Louisiana. The Mathis Trophy was awarded to the top crew in bombing and celestial navigation combined. Also in the picture are Flt Lt Patrick Langdown (front, left) and his crew, who won the Navigation Trophy.

Bottom:
Vulcan flypast over its old rival, the B-52.

the more sophisticated equipment carried by the B-52s and F-111s was expected to carry the day. In the event, 'We did what everybody said couldn't be done — beat Strategic Air Command in the USA.' These words came from a delighted AVM David Evans, AOC 1 Group, whose four Vulcan crews had lined up at Barksdale, Louisiana against the top crews from every SAC B-52 and F-111 wing bar one. There were four basic missions for all 51 aircraft including one high altitude and four low-level simulated bomb releases, plus a low-level navigation route through Mississippi, Louisiana and Arkansas.

Nothing demonstrated the change since Pinecastle more vividly than AVM Evans' statement that, 'The Americans have been impressed with the professionalism of our crews.' The best example of this came on the last mission, before which the No 101 Squadron crew, captained by Flt Lt Patrick Langdown, was lying second by one point in the navigation stakes. On boarding the aircraft the crew discovered that two pieces of primary navigation equipment were unserviceable; thus there was no updating facility in the entire system and all navigation had to be done 'manually'. On a normal training mission in the UK the crew would almost certainly have aborted, but they elected to fly and turned in the best navigation score of the competition to win the Navigation Trophy. 'I don't believe in good luck,' said AVM Evans. 'You can only *make* good luck for yourself.'

But pride of place in the competition went to Flt Lt Peter Perry and his No 230 OCU crew. Pete Perry, who had progressed from being the youngest V-bomber captain in 1961 to teaching Prince Charles to fly the Vulcan in 1971, took off from Barksdale on the final competition sortie knowing that if his crew could place their bomb within 200ft they would win. Unfortunately they lost their best navigation aids en route and the nav

team had to go back to basics, but that was what the Vulcan training schedule was all about and the bomb was spot on. For the first and only time, the RAF won the prestigious Mathis Trophy for the top crew in bombing and celestial navigation combined, and in so doing the Vulcan proved conclusively that it was still good enough to beat the Americans at their own game in their own backyard.

'We did it all by crew co-operation,' concluded Peter Perry, and that was the key to the Vulcan's success. 'I would have been happy to get airborne at any time to go to war in a Vulcan. A determined crew who routed the right way, who flew very low-level very fast, and who knew what they were going for, would get there without doubt. All targets are possible provided you have got the right crew behind you.'

As if to reinforce Pete Perry's point, selected Vulcan crews from 1977 onwards took part in the toughest peacetime training exercise of all, 'Red Flag' in Nevada. Red Flag was set up by the USAF to retain its 'seasoned' combat capability after Vietnam, and it was conducted over a range approaching the size of Switzerland against targets ranging from trucks to industrial complexes protected by simulated Soviet missile defences and experienced fighter pilots flying F-5s to Warsaw Pact rules.

'Each Vulcan crew flew five sorties,' recorded a Buccaneer Wing Commander after the first Vulcan deployment to Nevada in 1977.

'At first we were amazed how they seemed to be gluttons for punishment. Flying high-low-high profiles, they began the exercise by flying through the gauntlet of range defences twice per sortie. Initially they operated at 300ft above ground level where, despite casting the inevitable large triangular shadows on the desert floor, they performed very well in evading most air and ground threats. Later in the exercise, when cleared down to 200ft, they used terrain masking and three-axis jinking

more effectively; frequently they survived without a single claim being verified against them. To do this in the unlimited visibility of Nevada was no mean achievement, and they impressed all by their professionalism.'

There was no higher praise than that. But all good things have to come to an end. As the swept-wing and swept-up Tornado entered service to take over the Vulcans' tactical strike responsibilities in NATO, No 230 OCU disbanded first on 31 August 1981 followed by No 617 Squadron at the end of the year. '617's' last Vulcan mission was flown by XL318 on 11 December 1981 along the Derwent Reservoir route which the squadron had used to practise for the 1943 Dams Raid — XL318 now represents the Vulcan family at Gibraltar.

Nos 35 and 27 Squadrons followed suit at the end of February and March 1982 respectively, and the intention was to phase out No 9 Squadron at the end of April followed by Nos 44, 50 and 101 Squadrons on 30 June. But at the 11th hour the Argentinians, who coincidentally had approached Britain in 1981 to enquire whether surplus Vulcans could be purchased to replace the Canberra in Argentinian Air Force service, invaded the Falkland Islands on 2 April 1982. No 9 Squadron disbanded on schedule but the retirement plans for the last three Vulcan units were put in abeyance as the delta bomber prepared to do battle for real for the first and last time.

It is one of the interesting footnotes of history that among the first overseas flag-waving missions ever undertaken by the Vulcan was one to Buenos Aires in 1958. Dr Arturo Frondisi had become the first elected Argentinian president in 12 years, and

Below:
Flt Lt Les Aylott and his No 101 Squadron crew take off from Nellis AFB, Nevada, on Exercise 'Red Flag' — the Sunrise Mountains in the background are typical Nevada terrain.

on 1 May two Vulcans flew an airborne salute over the Inauguration Ceremony. Democracy had disappeared 25 years later and, while a British Task Force was setting out to retake the Falklands, Vulcan attentions turned once more to the South Atlantic.

Waddington was then the only remaining Vulcan base, and the order to prepare for possible operations went out on 9 April (Good Friday): Wg Cdr Simon Baldwin, OC No 44 Squadron, was suddenly recalled from his Easter leave to become OC Vulcan Falklands effort. He was allowed to choose his support personnel so he roped in the experts from the Waddington Operations Wing planning staff — men like Sqn Ldr John Williams, a Nav Radar who had been on No 1 Vulcan OCU Course back in 1957 and who had been dropping bombs from Vulcans before some of the current aircrew had been born. Extra telephones were installed in the Waddington conference room and Simon Baldwin's team set about planning the furthest-ranging bombing mission in history.

Waddington's brief was to produce a long-range conventional bombing capability with up to 10 aircraft as soon as possible. There were no inhibitions about bombing military targets in the Falklands, and though there was no firm objective at this stage, the planning team assumed that the Vulcans would be sent against the runway at Port Stanley. The Service Chiefs were particularly worried about the air threat to the Task Force, and the Argentinians had to be prevented or dissuaded from deploying their Skyhawks, Mirages and Super Etendards into Port Stanley.

With this in mind, Waddington's first task was to identify the best airframes for use over the South Atlantic. Given the distances involved — some 4,100 miles from Waddington to the staging post at Ascension Island, and another 3,900 miles from Ascension to the Falklands — a serviceable flight refuelling system was essential to top up en route from Victor tankers. Although each Vulcan B.2 had an air-to-air refuelling capability, it had been blanked off and the 'plumbing' inhibited at the probe connection for over a decade. After non-return valves and dried-out seals were replaced, and pipes checked under pressure for leaks, 10 Vulcans were declared up to standard.

From the start it was assumed that Vulcan raids would take place at night to reduce the risk of interception. However, two weeks after Easter the Waddington engineers were asked to fit an electronic countermeasures pod to the Vulcan as a number of ground-to-air radars had arrived in the Falklands. The only pod readily available was the Buccaneers' Westinghouse AN/ALQ-101 pod — known as the Dash Ten pod — and this could only be fitted to one of the twin Skybolt hard-points under the wings of the 300-series engined Vulcans.

Above:
Two Vulcan B.1s, formating on a Comet of Transport Command, overfly Buenos Aires in 1958 — the trio subsequently flew a 'bomb break' over the Plazo de Mayo where President Frondisi was standing after his inauguration. The Vulcans' 14,000-mile round trip to Argentina via Dakar and Rio without any unserviceability proved that the delta was truly 'a global bomber'. It was a lesson the Argentinians had forgotten 24 years later.

Below:
1,000lb HE bombs about to be loaded at Wideawake airfield, Ascension. Trials were carried out in May with laser guided bombs but, despite their pinpoint accuracy, LGBs sported very big fins and as the Vulcan could only carry three of them, they were rejected in favour of good old free-fall bombs. *Crown Copyright*

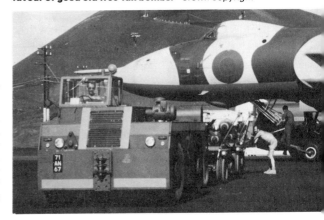

The pool of available Vulcans was thereby reduced to five, (XL391, XM597, XM598, XM607, XM612) and all these were then fitted with Carousel for additional navigation accuracy. Carousel was a twin inertial navigation system originally installed in the ex-British Airways Super VC10s then being stored at Abingdon awaiting conversion to tankers. Carousel was essential if the Vulcans were to navigate accurately over great stretches of water miles away from identifiable land features, and an inertial navigator kept the NBS free for bombing runs only.

These aircraft were then left to the engineers to hone to perfection. Their Olympus 301 engines, which had previously been limited to 98% power to extend service life, were restored to full thrust. As the Vulcan had been operated exclusively in the nuclear role during recent years, the carriers and controls had to be changed to accommodate 21 1,000lb HE bombs. The co-pilot received an additional radar altimeter, and a triple offset radar fit — designed for greater accuracy in bombing competitions by enabling three offset points to be used during a bombing run — was installed. There was an element of good fortune here because the triple offset boxes had to be rescued from a skip at Scampton where they were about to be scrapped. The aircraft were then 'tweaked' and calibrated to work as accurately as their elderly components and design specification would allow. XM597 and XM607 eventually proved themselves to be the best bombers — 'the aircraft chose themselves,' said Simon Baldwin.

Three crews were initially selected to complement the aircraft — Sqn Ldr John Reeve's crew from No 50 Squadron, Flt Lt Martin Withers' crew from No 101 Squadron and Sqn Ldr 'Monty' Montgomery's crew from No 44 Squadron. Experience was the key to crew selection with two out of three crews having recent 'Red Flag' experience, but all had much to learn when it came to in-flight refuelling and iron bomb dropping.

Airborne flight refuelling training began on 13 April, and each crew was to complete three refuellings (known as 'prods') by day and two by night. Air-to-air refuelling instructors (AARIs) from the Victor tanker OCU at Marham were initially attached to each Vulcan crew to give instruction. The AARIs were particularly valuable because none of the bomber pilots had experience of tanker formation techniques, but when it became clear that there would only be time to train Vulcan captains and not co-pilots, it was decided to retain the AARIs on the bombing missions. The AARI would sit in the co-pilot's seat and fly or supervise the 'prods' all the way down to the Falklands. The co-pilot sat in the sixth seat, and after the final 'prod' he would swap seats with the AARI for the bomb run; afterwards they would

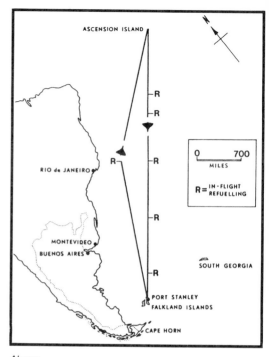

Above:
Vulcan route, with in-flight refuelling points, flown by Flt Lt Withers and his crew on 'Black Buck 1'.

swap seats again for the return leg. This arrangement made a lot of sense because it relieved the strain on the captain who would need all his wits about him for the attack, and it provided a valuable reserve capability in case the captain was incapacitated.

The pressure was on to train the bomber crews as quickly as possible because it was clear that as soon as they got it right, they would go. Weekends went by the board and the three crews flew 50 hours in 10 days, of which 70% was at night. The bombing side was no great problem. Crews flew routes round the Western Scottish Isles to gain experience in long sea legs with little land crossing, and they came down progressively to 300ft above the darkened waves relying on terrain-following radar. Apart from overcoming the fear factor in operating so close to the ground without visual reference, much of the training was spent calibrating kit and on conventional bombing practice at Garvie and Jurby Ranges so that Nav Radars became familiar with their equipment and conventional arming procedures — 'we didn't want to go all that way and drop safe bombs'.

Having become proficient in conventional bombing and in-flight refuelling, there was only the problem of fuel leaks to overcome, which was easier said than done. Unlike the Victor, where the receiver probe is mounted above the cockpit like a unicorn horn, the Vulcan probe was in the nose below the cockpit. The first few Vulcan 'prods' over the UK revealed that fuel leaked out of the probe and back over the windscreen. The airflow over the nose kept it on the windscreen — the wipers could not clear it and the moisture totally obscured the view forward which did nothing for accurate station-keeping with the tanker ahead. A colander was placed around the probe base to disperse the fuel, but to no avail. Then deflector blades were fitted on the nose to break up the airflow keeping the fuel in place, but this 'fix' did not really work either.

As if these slight leaks were not bad enough, very large spillages also occurred. These monster gushes were a menace because a large leak could cause the engines to flame-out; several double-engine flame-outs resulted and 'Monty' Montgomery suffered a particularly nasty one at night. All was gloom and despondency by 24 April because no matter how adept the crews became at bombing, if they could not take fuel on board safely, they would never get near their target.

Fortunately on 25 April it all came right. Leaks were reduced to a minimum when it was found that the original Vulcan refuelling valves were not assembled to specification. A helicopter was dispatched to Marham to pick up some Victor probes which had been fitted to different standards, and these did the trick. The Chief of Air Staff came down to Waddington, and asked, 'Can you do it?' Waddington's answer was yes, though they could give no guarantees. That was good enough, and on 29 April XM597 and XM607 deployed to Ascension Island.

Sqn Ldr Montgomery was nominated as detachment commander and his crew became the operations crew at Ascension, leaving the Reeve and Withers crews to fly the missions. Vulcan operations against the Falklands were code-named 'Black Buck', and it was planned that crews would fly the nine-hour trip to Ascension, get eight hours sleep, and go to it. Thus at 10.50pm Ascension time (7.50pm Port Stanley time) on 30 April, 10 supporting Victor tankers (plus one reserve) roared off at one-minute intervals from Ascension followed by two Vulcans. John Reeve captained the primary crew in XM597 for the particular reason that his Nav Radar, Flt Lt Mick Cooper, had previous experience of conventional bombing. XM607 was the reserve Vulcan captained by Martin Withers, but as they climbed upwards the Withers' crew heard the news that XM597 had to turn back because the cabin could not be pressurised. Instead of being back in at Ascension in four hours, the Withers crew with AARI Flt Lt Dick Russell was now faced with a 16-hour flight sustained only by sandwiches and flasks of hot coffee. It was a fortuitous occurrence because XM607 had the better bombing kit, and 'Black Buck 1' set off in mass formation with the 10 Victors needed to get it to the Falklands.

Vulcan flight time from Ascension to Port Stanley was over eight hours and, if a crow could have managed it, the shortest distance each way was 3,886 miles. The first fuel transfer took place about 1¾ hours after take-off at a point 840 miles south of Ascension. Four Victors topped up the tanks of four others before turning back, and this 'cascade' refuelling plan was repeated a number of times until only one Victor remained with the bomber. Unfortunately by the time the solitary pair were an hour away from Port Stanley, it had become clear that fuel consumption was considerably higher than forecast. Part of the reason was that despite its long record of service, the 'Black Buck' Vulcan was operating into the unknown. Take-off weight had been 210,000lb, compared with the normal maximum of 204,000lb, and the Dash Ten pod was causing extra drag under the starboard wing. Moreover, because the heavily laden Victors could not reach the optimum Vulcan cruising height around 40,000ft, the Vulcan had to stay around 30,000ft to keep formation with the tankers, which increased fuel consumption still further on the long flight south. Finally, the crucial Victor tasked to top up the Vulcan prior to attack broke its probe while itself taking on fuel in turbulent conditions. The Victor donor immediately reversed roles with the damaged tanker, taking back its fuel from the latter before transitting to rendezvous with the Vulcan. Thus, when XM607 refuelled for the last time six hours after leaving Ascension, Martin Withers found himself some 6,000lb short of fuel he should have had at this time, and the donating Victor had sacrificed so much that it would need a tanker itself to get home. As Withers throttled back to begin descent 290 miles north of the target, his crew was relying more than ever on meeting a Victor on the return journey.

As the Vulcan had only enough fuel to get in and out in a straight line, the Waddington planners had gone for a low-level penetration to maximise surprise and thereby minimise warning time to launch land-based interceptors. Consequently, as the Vulcan levelled out at 2,000ft over the sea at a point 233 miles from the target, it was well below Argentinian radar cover. From there Withers made a gentle descent to 300ft to make doubly sure that no prying electronic eyes would see the Vulcan coming. There was only one imponderable remaining — having left Ascension eight hours earlier, and having both flown a route far away from ground fixes and maintained radio and radar silence to mask the approach, Nav Plotter Flt Lt Gordon Graham could only hope that the

Carousel inertial navigator lived up to expectations.

The attack profile against Port Stanley runway was determined by two major factors — the need to crater the runway and, where possible, to avoid the Argentinian defences. At this stage in the conflict, Britain could ill-afford the morale-denting loss of a Vulcan, so XM607's best chance of coming through unscathed was to approach the target at low level at night. Given meteorological predictions of strong winds, low cloud and severe turbulence, together with the lack of guiding lights around the airfield, the planners had no choice but to opt for a radar attack. At first glance, the best way of closing a runway is to start at the threshold and drop a stick of 21 1,000lb bombs all the way down it. Unfortunately, there are errors in every system, and only the slightest misjudgement could result in a neat line of bomb craters parallel to the runway and much Argentinian merriment all round. So the best statistical chance of hitting the runway was to fly across it at an angle of 35° and release the bombs in a line at ¼-second (50yd) intervals. This approach and stick spacing would never put all 21 bombs on the runway but, given the known errors in the Vulcan bombing system, it stood a 95% chance of putting at least one bomb on the runway. Thus, as it approached the east-west runway at Port Stanley, XM607 was on an attack track of 235°.

As the range to target came down to below 60 miles, the Nav Radar, Flt Lt Bob Wright, finally turned on his H2S radar which up to then had lain dormant to prevent warning emissions. There was no sign of the expected return from Mount Usborne in the middle of East Falkland but as Martin Withers eased the Vulcan up to 500ft to widen the radar horizon, the mountain suddenly appeared exactly where it should be. The Carousel combined with Gordon Graham's astro-navigation had the Vulcan almost exactly on track; more ominously, the crew received a further position check when the passive warning receiver started to pick up signals from the TPS-43 early-warning radar at Port Stanley.

A conventional bomb dropped from 500ft may well bounce and at best cause a crater only 12ft wide by 3ft deep, which would not put a runway out of action for long. A bomb dropped from above 2,000ft however would have time to reach terminal velocity and drive into the runway; with a delayed action use it could then produce a crater 65ft wide and up to 20ft deep.

But 'Black Buck 1' could not overfly at 2,000ft because of the Argentinian defences. The planners knew that the enemy had Tigercat anti-aircraft missiles, which were potent by day up to 8,500ft, and Oerlikon 35mm fast-firing twin-barrelled guns linked in some cases to Skyguard or Super Fledermaus fire-control radars. The elderly Tigercat was the least dangerous but the Oerlikon was a greater threat up to 6,500ft. The nastiest opponent of all was the Roland anti-aircraft missile which was a threat up to 16,000ft. Bombing from 20,000ft would have degraded accuracy so it was a great relief to the planning team and crews when it was discovered shortly before the raid that Roland was probably not at Port Stanley.

With 46 miles to go, therefore, Martin Withers pulled the Vulcan into a rapid climb to 10,000ft. This attack height was designed to overfly Tigercat and the Oerlikons, give Bob Wright more time to identify his aiming offsets and ensure maximum penetration of the runway by the 1,000lb bombs. There was ⅝ cloud over the Falklands that night and although the outline of the island could be clearly seen through gaps in the cloud, the airfield could not be relied upon to give a good radar return and Bob Wright used nearby ground features as his offsets.

As they ran in at 320kts, Withers and his co-pilot, Flg Off Pete Taylor, expected the Argentinian defences to open up at any moment. The bomb doors were opened 10 miles from the target and Withers waited expectantly for the flak and perhaps missiles, but nothing happened. It was perhaps misleading to say that the enemy was caught well and truly napping — the AEO, Flt Lt Hugh Prior, certainly heard the high-pitched scratching note of a Skyguard fire-control radar on his radar warning receiver.

Finally, about two miles short of the runway, the bombing computer signalled bomb release. A single nuclear bomb is gone in the blinking of an eye but Martin Withers had to maintain a very steady straight and level bombing platform while all 21 bombs went on their way. They were gone in five seconds but to the crew 'it seemed like an age'.

It took about 20 seconds for the bombs to hit the ground, by which time Withers was hauling the delta round and into a full power climb. As he looked out of the cockpit window in the eerie silence, co-pilot Taylor suddenly saw the clouds over the airfield light up from below; as the darkness returned, the crew felt the distant crump of explosions merging together.

The South Atlantic dawn was breaking as the bomber reached top of climb and Hugh Prior sent the single codeword 'Superfuse' to report a successful attack. But the Vulcan was still not out of the woods. Reduced fuel transfer at the final inbound rendezvous made an early link-up with a Victor tanker essential. In the event, with a Nimrod monitoring the area well south of the planned point, contact was made in good time. As he saw the underside of the Victor swinging into position, Withers thought it was 'the most beautiful sight in the world'.

Unfortunately, not only did precious fuel start to flow into the tanks but it also flooded back over the Vulcan's windscreen as well. Even with the wipers going full chat, Withers could only see the blurred outline of the tanker in front. He could not afford to break contact because he might never regain it, but fortunately Bob Wright had come forward to watch the operation from the ladder between the pilots' steps and he noticed a narrow strip at the base of the centre windscreen that remained clear. Through this he gave a running commentary on the tanker's position, which enabled the pilot to hold station. It took 10 fraught minutes to fill the Vulcan's tanks with sufficient fuel to get back to Ascension, and only then could contact be broken. Immediately the airflow cleared the spillage and all

was sunshine and blue skies in the Vulcan cockpit. It was time to go home.

Now that the dust has settled, how should we judge the Vulcan's performance on 1 May 1982? Most Vulcan men were not surprised that the bomber managed to get to Port Stanley and back, though it was the first time that a Vulcan crew had flown in such a large formation at night. The Vulcan, though long in the tooth, was a hardy old warhorse, and once the cobwebs were blown out of the in-flight refuelling system and the kit updated, she was more than capable of living up to the world-wide capability called for in the original specification. Avro's bomber had stood the test of time.

Where most Vulcan men were surprised was in the accuracy of bomb delivery on Port Stanley runway. Given that the Vulcan's radar bombing system was designed 30 years earlier, and that the specification only called for a bombing accuracy of 440yd at low level, there are not many bookmakers who would have given reasonable odds on hitting a target as small and narrow as a runway obscured by cloud in total darkness. In the event, Bob Wright and his kit dropped with no line error whatsoever, which was not only almost unheard of but was also a tremendous tribute to the groundcrew who tweaked the bombing system to perfection. 'It all went smoothly, like training,' said Bob Wright, but those modest words said it all — the Vulcan and its crews had always trained for war, and when the war came, neither aircraft nor men let Britain down.

The first bomb in the stick hit the centre of Port Stanley runway, and other bombs hit a small hangar, a store dump by the control tower, and closed the only road to Stanley which caused the enemy a great deal of trouble because their

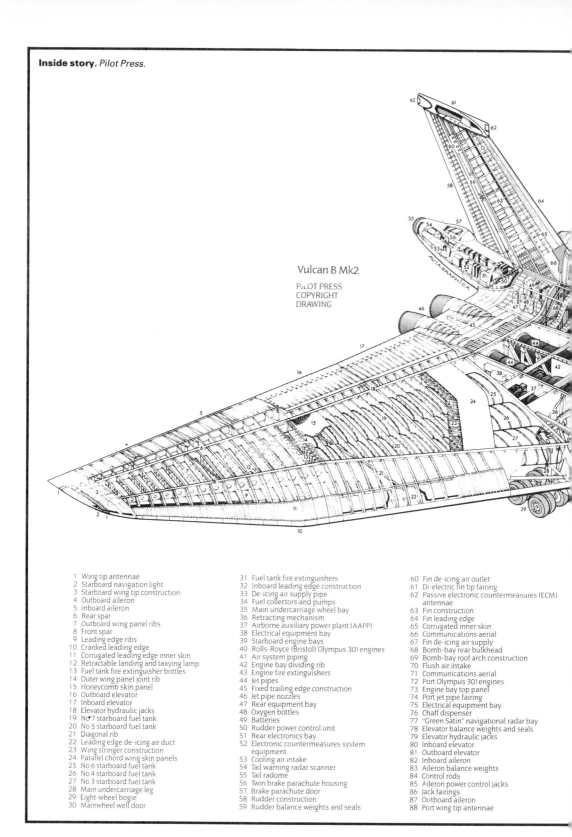

Vulcan B Mk2

PILOT PRESS
COPYRIGHT
DRAWING

1 Wing tip antennae
2 Starboard navigation light
3 Starboard wing tip construction
4 Outboard aileron
5 Inboard aileron
6 Rear spar
7 Outboard wing panel ribs
8 Front spar
9 Leading edge ribs
10 Cranked leading edge
11 Corrugated leading edge inner skin
12 Retractable landing and taxying lamp
13 Fuel tank fire extinguisher bottles
14 Outer wing panel joint rib
15 Honeycomb skin panel
16 Outboard elevator
17 Inboard elevator
18 Elevator hydraulic jacks
19 No 7 starboard fuel tank
20 No 5 starboard fuel tank
21 Diagonal rib
22 Leading edge de-icing air duct
23 Wing stringer construction
24 Parallel chord wing skin panels
25 No 6 starboard fuel tank
26 No 4 starboard fuel tank
27 No 3 starboard fuel tank
28 Main undercarriage leg
29 Eight-wheel bogie
30 Mainwheel well door

31 Fuel tank fire extinguishers
32 Inboard leading edge construction
33 De-icing air supply pipe
34 Fuel collectors and pumps
35 Main undercarriage wheel bay
36 Retracting mechanism
37 Airborne auxiliary power plant (AAPP)
38 Electrical equipment bay
39 Starboard engine bays
40 Rolls-Royce (Bristol) Olympus 301 engines
41 Air system piping
42 Engine bay dividing rib
43 Engine fire extinguishers
44 Jet pipes
45 Fixed trailing edge construction
46 Jet pipe nozzles
47 Rear equipment bay
48 Oxygen bottles
49 Batteries
50 Rudder power control unit
51 Rear electronics bay
52 Electronic countermeasures system
    equipment
53 Cooling air intake
54 Tail warning radar scanner
55 Tail radome
56 Twin brake parachute housing
57 Brake parachute door
58 Rudder construction
59 Rudder balance weights and seals

60 Fin de-icing air outlet
61 Di-electric fin tip fairing
62 Passive electronic countermeasures (ECM)
    antennae
63 Fin construction
64 Fin leading edge
65 Corrugated inner skin
66 Communications aerial
67 Fin de-icing air supply
68 Bomb-bay rear bulkhead
69 Bomb-bay roof arch construction
70 Flush air intake
71 Communications aerial
72 Port Olympus 301 engines
73 Engine bay top panel
74 Port jet pipe fairing
75 Electrical equipment bay
76 Chaff dispenser
77 "Green Satin" navigational radar bay
78 Elevator balance weights and seals
79 Elevator hydraulic jacks
80 Inboard elevator
81 Outboard elevator
82 Inboard aileron
83 Aileron balance weights
84 Control rods
85 Aileron power control jacks
86 Jack fairings
87 Outboard aileron
88 Port wing tip antennae

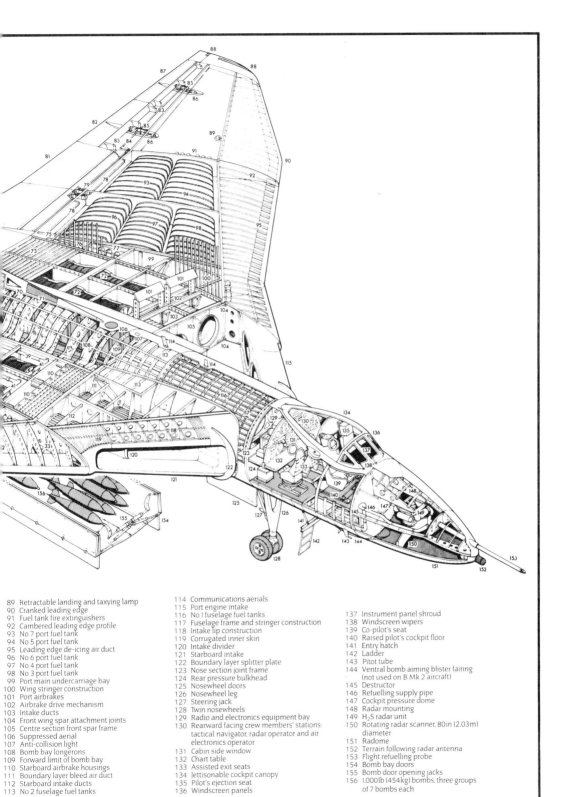

89 Retractable landing and taxying lamp
90 Cranked leading edge
91 Fuel tank fire extinguishers
92 Cambered leading edge profile
93 No 7 port fuel tank
94 No 5 port fuel tank
95 Leading edge de-icing air duct
96 No 6 port fuel tank
97 No 4 port fuel tank
98 No 3 port fuel tank
99 Port main undercarriage bay
100 Wing stringer construction
101 Port airbrakes
102 Airbrake drive mechanism
103 Intake ducts
104 Front wing spar attachment joints
105 Centre section front spar frame
106 Suppressed aerial
107 Anti-collision light
108 Bomb bay longerons
109 Forward limit of bomb bay
110 Starboard airbrake housings
111 Boundary layer bleed air duct
112 Starboard intake ducts
113 No 2 fuselage fuel tanks

114 Communications aerials
115 Port engine intake
116 No 1 fuselage fuel tanks
117 Fuselage frame and stringer construction
118 Intake lip construction
119 Corrugated inner skin
120 Intake divider
121 Starboard intake
122 Boundary layer splitter plate
123 Nose section joint frame
124 Rear pressure bulkhead
125 Nosewheel doors
126 Nosewheel leg
127 Steering jack
128 Twin nosewheels
129 Radio and electronics equipment bay
130 Rearward facing crew members' stations:
    tactical navigator, radar operator and air
    electronics operator
131 Cabin side window
132 Chart table
133 Assisted exit seats
134 Jettisonable cockpit canopy
135 Pilot's ejection seat
136 Windscreen panels

137 Instrument panel shroud
138 Windscreen wipers
139 Co-pilot's seat
140 Raised pilot's cockpit floor
141 Entry hatch
142 Ladder
143 Pitot tube
144 Ventral bomb aiming blister fairing
    (not used on B Mk 2 aircraft)
145 Destructor
146 Refuelling supply pipe
147 Cockpit pressure dome
148 Radar mounting
149 H₂S radar unit
150 Rotating radar scanner, 80in (2.03m)
    diameter
151 Radome
152 Terrain following radar antenna
153 Flight refuelling probe
154 Bomb bay doors
155 Bomb door opening jacks
156 1,000lb (454kg) bombs, three groups
    of 7 bombs each

vehicles then sank into the mud on either side. A lot of rubbish has been written about the futility of flying 8,000 miles to drop so few bombs, especially as Argentinian Hercules transport aircraft flew into Port Stanley until the end. But this criticism misses the point. A Hercules is designed to operate from small strips and it would have taken many repeat sorties to deny the airfield permanently to the enemy. What the Vulcan was sent to do, and did most successfully, was to deny Port Stanley runway to the Skyhawks, Mirages and Super Etendards which could have crippled the Task

Force on the San Carlos beaches had they been based at cockpit readiness on the island. Just as the sinking of the *General Belgrano* kept the enemy Navy in port, so 'Black Buck 1' disrupted the airfield and kept the most potent aircraft in the Argentinian inventory back on the mainland and at the limits of their operating range.

In addition the raid forced the enemy to disperse Pucara aircraft and logistical supplies away from Port Stanley airfield, and to divert troops to defend them by day and by night. 'Black Buck 1' also sustained national morale and gave hope to the Falkland Islanders for the first time in a month. Finally, it convinced the Argentinian Junta that the British were committed to an all-out military effort and obliquely served notice on Buenos Aires not to escalate the conflict because the RAF had the capability to attack airfields on the mainland if it was forced to do so. All in all, this and the later Vulcan raids had a significant impact on the successful outcome of the war out of all proportion to the destruction wrought, and after a flight lasting 15hr 45min, the whole Black Buck 1 Vulcan crew was Mentioned in Dispatches. Martin Withers was also to be awarded the DFC for his leadership, determination and presence of mind which inspired his crew on a mission fraught with potential hazards beyond enemy action.

With the first 'Black Buck' judged to be a success, 'Black Buck 2' was launched late in the evening of 3 May. XM607 was back in action having proved itself to be the best bomber, and bomb load and target were the same as before, but this time Sqn Ldr Reeve and his crew were to be given their chance. The lessons of the first raid had been taken to heart, and major changes were made to the refuelling procedures which worked very well. As the Roland missile was now believed to be in the Falklands, John Reeve flew the bomb run at 16,000ft. Again XM607 performed very well and there was no aircraft error, but this time the stick of bombs narrowly missed the western edge of the runway.

The Vulcan could have struck again very quickly but 'Black Bucks' were highly tanker intensive and, as Argentinian diesel submarines were feared to be on patrol, tanker priority was given to Nimrod anti-submarine missions. However, a further attack — 'Black Buck 3' — was planned for 16 May against the runway, but strong forecast headwinds threatened to reduce fuel reserves below acceptable limits and the raid was cancelled before take-off. It was probably fortunate because the element of surprise had gone — it was time to seek other targets with other weapons.

Back at Waddington in the hectic latter half of April, a whole variety of Vulcan operational loads had been considered. When the Dash Ten pod was fitted under the starboard wing, it seemed sensible to carry something on the balancing Skybolt point under the port wing and the first candidate was Sidewinder. The new AIM-9L version of this heat-seeking missile was to win its spurs in Harrier service in the conflict, and feasibility studies were carried out to fit two Sidewinders on the port pylon for Vulcan self-defence. No Sidewinders were test-fired though there was a fleeting suggestion that a Vulcan so equipped might take out the Boeing 707 that the enemy was using in the airborne early-warning role over the South Atlantic.

Of all the novel loads proposed, the one that found the most operational favour was the anti-radar missile. An anti-radar missile is designed to home on to transmissions from enemy radars and, as the Argentinians were using their Falklands-based Westinghouse TPS-43 radar to direct air raids against the Task Force and to warn their own aircraft of Harrier patrols, it was decided to try and put out these radar eyes as a matter of urgency. The same priority was also applied to the Oerlikon gun-laying control radars.

The anti-radar Martel was the first choice of weapon because it was currently in service with the Buccaneer, and XM597 was adapted to carry a single round on the port pylon. Two flight trials were then carried out on 4 and 5 May; the latter was a live firing over the Aberporth range after a cold soak at altitude because there was some doubt about Martel's performance at the end of a high-altitude mission.

Eventually Martel was rejected in favour of the American Shrike anti-radar missile. One missile was fitted initially but then the US Navy twin-launcher was adopted. It was then decided to dispense with the Dash Ten pod on Shrike missions, enabling four missiles to be carried. The whole flight fitment and trials programme was repeated for Shrike and the weapon went from concept to operational use in just 10 days.

As all three primary Vulcan crews were needed to plan and execute the conventional bombing raids, Sqn Ldr Neil McDougall's crew from No 50 Squadron was nominated to work up for anti-radar missile duties. It deployed to Ascension on 27 May with XM597 as its primary aircraft and XM598 as reserve.

'Black Buck 4' was to have been the first anti-radar sortie but the mission — planned for 29 May — was aborted when the refuelling hose motor on one of the tankers went unserviceable before the penultimate 'prod'. XM597 and the McDougall crew were back in the air on 'Black Buck 5' the following evening. As the Vulcan carried no bombs, it had room for the two bomb-bay tanks which normally surrounded a nuclear weapon, thereby increasing fuel capacity by 16,000lb and simplifying the airborne refuelling

Above:
A pair of Shrike missiles under the wing of XM597. The makeshift missile pylons were initially made from mild steel girders which happened to be on hand at Waddington, though they were slightly refined later by the St Athan Maintenance Unit. No further anti-radiation missile work was undertaken with the Vulcan after the Falklands. *Crown Copyright*

requirement to four 'prods' on the outbound leg. Like its predecessors, 'Black Buck 5' approached Port Stanley at low level before climbing to 16,000ft to attack the TPS-43 radar while Harriers were simultaneously attacking the airfield. Unfortunately, the McDougall crew was not helped by not knowing exactly which Argentinian radar the missiles had locked on to. XM597 only carried two Shrikes on this mission and they were very range critical — accuracy fell off above seven miles from the target. Moreover, because of the rigid nature of the missile's seeker mounting, Shrike had to be pointed directly at the TPS-43 target at launch: the AEO, Flt Lt Rod Trevaskus, had to call out changes of heading from an instrumentation console very similar to an ILS system with azimuth and elevation bars.

Consequently, even though Shrike picked up the TPS-43 on the way in, the radar was switched off a few minutes later and Neil McDougall had to fly a complex pattern around the island trying to get into the right attack position again. After 40 minutes Travaskus detected the radar again, whereupon McDougall flew north and then swung round to ripple-launch both Shrikes. The missiles disappeared into the cloud below, but although flashes were seen on the ground, the radar must have been switched off at the crucial moment because the TPS-43 escaped serious damage.

Three days later the McDougall crew flew XM597 on another defence suppression mission.

This time the Vulcan carried four Shrikes — two pre-tuned for the TPS-43 and the other pair optimised against the gun-laying radars. Once more the Vulcan approached from the northeast at low level and then popped up to 16,000ft, but by now the Argentinians knew what to expect. As 'Black Buck 6' got to about nine miles from Port Stanley, the radars went off, only to come back on again once the Vulcan flew past. This cat and mouse game continued for 40 minutes and, as the time came for a final run before having to go home, McDougall decided to dive towards the airfield to try and tempt some reaction. The ploy worked, and as XM597 approached 10,000ft, one of the radars came on and guns started firing. Rod Trevaskus was able to lock on two Shrikes, off they went, and one blast/fragmentation warhead detonated close to a Skyguard fire control radar, crumpling the van and killing three of the operating crew.

McDougall climbed away but on the return leg his refuelling probe broke, necessitating an emergency diversion into Rio de Janeiro. Unfortunately, with barely 3,000lb fuel remaining in his tanks, and needing 2,500lb to fly a circuit, he found himself four miles high only six miles from the runway. With superb skill he racked the giant delta round into an almost vertical bank and a steep descending orbit to bleed off height and eventually

Below:
Farewell flypast by four Vulcans of No 44 Squadron on 21 December 1982 just before the Squadron disbanded. XM607, the bomber of Port Stanley airfield, is in the lead while the Shrike carrier, XM597, brings up the rear. XM 612 (foreground) and XL391 complete the quartet. *Lawrence*

make a perfect landing; he did not even need to stream the tail chute to bring the bomber to a halt on the short runway. It was a wonderful achievement by both man and machine, and Neil McDougall deserved his subsequent award of the DFC for a superb demonstration of flying skill.

By now the British forces were firmly ashore in the Falklands and 'yomping' towards Stanley. RAF long-range bombing thoughts now turned towards helping the troops in their final push, and on 12 June, at the same time as the McDougall crew belatedly returned after their seven-day sojourn in Brazil, Martin Withers and his crew took-off on the seventh and final 'Black Buck'. This time the aim was to cause maximum damage to 'soft' targets such as aircraft and vehicles in the general area of Port Stanley airfield, and XM607 was armed with iron bombs fused to 'air burst' and scatter lethal fragments everywhere. Apart from an engine flame-out which took three attempts to relight, the mission was uneventful. Two days later the Argentinian commander on the island surrendered.

So ended the most complex and longest-ranging bombing missions in the history of military aviation. The distance from Ascension to the Falklands was the equivalent of flying from Waddington to the Russo-Chinese border, and great credit must go to the engineers who made it all work, to the planners who came up with the goods from their memory banks, and to the aircrews who flew day in and day out in configurations few had ever experienced before and who put it all together when it mattered. And finally, all praise must go to the Vulcans themselves which did everything asked of them, and more, in the twilight of their existence.

11
The Eternal Triangle

For No 101 Squadron the Falklands conflict brought only a temporary respite and the Squadron disbanded on 4 August 1982. No 44 Squadron followed suit on 31 December, but for No 50 Squadron life went on. Although the blood-letting in the South Atlantic was over, the threat remained and a sizeable air-to-air refuelling requirement was still required to support the Falklands garrison.

At the time of the Argentinian invasion the RAF's tanker force consisted of 22 Victors, and although plans had been laid to convert an extra nine ex-commercial VC10s to three-point tankers, the first VC10 tanker would not be ready until 1984. Consequently, the provision of a stop-gap tanker became a top priority, and this in turn sired the last of the Vulcan variants, the Vulcan B Mk 2(K).

No 50 Squadron was therefore kept in being to operate six Vulcan tankers which supplemented the Victor force until the arrival of the VC10. No 50 Squadron inherited the best aircraft from the disbanded units, and it was a relatively simple task to fit a standard Flight Refuelling Ltd Mk 17 hose drum unit (HDU) in a rather ungainly box-like fairing under the rear fuselage. A third

bomb bay tank was also installed in place of the nuclear weapon to bring the total fuel capacity of the Vulcan B.2(K) to 96,000lb. Little work was needed to permit all the fuel either to be used by the Vulcan or given away, and voila, there was a low cost tanker force-multiplier. Such was the ease of conversion that British Aerospace (née Avro) was notified of the requirement for a Vulcan tanker on 30 April 1982, the first flight was made from Woodford on 18 June, and CA Release was obtained on 23 June, the same day that the first Vulcan B.2(K) returned to Waddington.

As on its Victor cousin, the Nav Radar was responsible for Vulcan fuel management during refuelling. No 50 Squadron had a complement of 10 crews for its six tankers which were primarily engaged in support of the UK air defence force thereby freeing Victors for the South Atlantic. Nevertheless, the Squadron retained a bombing capability in the shape of four Vulcan B.2s which survived alongside the six B.2(K) tankers to the end.

Below:
No 50 Squadron Vulcans refuel in the air. *Jenvey*

No 50 Squadron and the Vulcan finally retired together on 31 March 1984. The Vulcan B.2(K) could certainly have carried on after the first VC10 tanker entered service, but the delta had to go for the very simple reason that the Mk 17 HDU had been out of production for some years and the Vulcan HDUs were needed for the VC10s. No fewer than 42 airframes were sold for scrap for a total of £69,574, while 175 Olympus engines were knocked down for £350 each. Roy Chadwick would have smiled for they set fire to Guy Gibson's Dambuster Lancaster at Scampton in 1947, but at least the Vulcan survives on static display in places as far apart as Cyprus and California.

It is too early to come to a definitive conclusion on the life of the Vulcan. Built originally at a cost of over £1million each, or at least 10 times that amount at present day values, the Vulcan was very much a multi-role combat aircraft. In its time the Vulcan has been a high and low-level bomber, a tanker, a stand-off and anti-radar missile carrier, undertaken maritime radar reconnaissance and been mooted as an air defender. Avro also designed a bomb bay crate to turn it into a photo reconnaissance platform, but along with other conversion schemes this was never implemented. 'We like to think,' said John Sheraton, Assistant Chief Designer Vulcan in 1978, 'that we didn't get any of them accepted because the Vulcan was the best bomber.'

Above:
The instrument panel of Vulcan B.2(K) XH560, seen with the cockpit seats removed for clarity.
Bob Downey

Above right:
Hercules receiver's eye view of the Vulcan drogue. The electronic countermeasures equipment was removed from the Vulcan tail to accommodate the piping leading to the unattractive box-like fairing underneath, which housed the hose drum unit. This underslung HDU reduced ground clearance and therefore necessitated revised take-off and landing techniques. *Jenvey*

Right:
The last Vulcan 'scramble' took place at RAF Waddington on 14 March 1984 and comprised three B.2(K)s (XH560, XH561 and XJ825) and one B.2 (XL426 — nearest), all of No 50 Squadron.
Allan Burney

Below right:
XM597, a B.2 of No 50 Squadron, was also present at Waddington. *Allan Burney*

Despite being a winner in all eyes, the Vulcan was never exported to another air force. 'We had nibbles but no serious business,' recalled Gilbert Whitehead. The RAF was not keen anyway and when the Australians were offered the Vulcan in 1961 as an interim Canberra replacement leading on to the TSR.2, the deal floundered because the

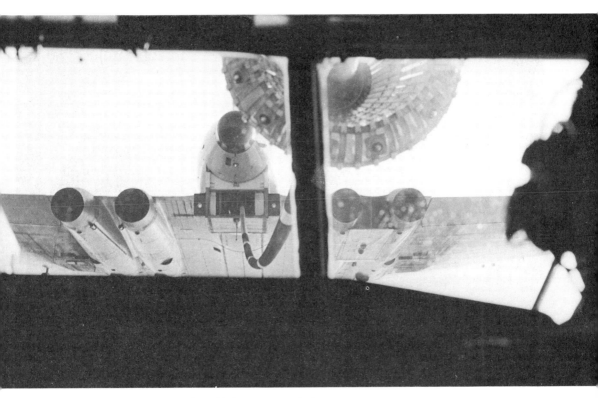

RAF insisted on retaining operational control.

It has to be said that unless one possessed a nuclear capability — and those few that did possessed their own aviation industries — a strategic bomber of the Vulcan class was a bit of an expensive luxury. Thus the Vulcan remained forever British. It was wholly British designed, built and operated, and the fact that the delta was but one of three excellent bombers built to meet an

Above:

The bitter end — XH557 and XJ784 on the Waddington scrap heap in December 1982. *Malcolm English*

Below:

The old and the new together — a Vulcan B.2(K) of No 50 Squadron about to tank a pair of Tornado GR.1s of No 9 Squadron in March 1984. *Gething*

independent strategic requirement may be contrasted with the Tornado GR.1 programme which has taken the combined efforts of *three* nations to produce *one* worthy successor to the Vulcan. The flying triangle may also prove to be eternal because the delta configuration is being proposed as a possible configuration for the next generation of USAF stealth bombers.

The *RAF Flying Review* for April 1963 stated that the 24 Blue Steels at Scampton had the equivalent striking power of three Polaris submarines, and that still left 46 Vulcans and 109 Valiants and Victors in reserve. As the Vulcan retired, taking with it a long range strategic bombing tradition stretching back to 1918, suffice to say that Great Britain made the Vulcan and the Vulcan made Britain great, and that will always remain its proudest epitaph.

Appendices — Vulcan Data

VULCAN DATA

Dimensions (ft/in)	B.1	B.1A	B.2
Overall length (nose to tail bullet)	92 9	99 11	99 11
Overall length (tip of refuelling probe to tail of radome)	—	105 6	105 6
Wing span	99 0	99 5	111 0
Height to top of fin	26 6	26 6	27 1
Wheel track	31 3	31 1	31 1
Wheel base	30 2	30 2	30 1½
Engines	4×Olympus 101, 102 or 104	4×Olympus 104	4×Olympus 200 series or Mk 301
Speed limitations	300kt/0.98M	300kt/0.95M	300kt/0.93M — 200 series 300kt/0.92M — Mk 301
Weight limitatations			
Maximum for take-off	167,000lb	167,000lb	204,000lb
Normal landing	125,000lb	125,000lb	140,000lb
Emergency landing	167,000lb	167,000lb	204,000lb

AVRO 707 DATA

	707	707B	707A	707C
Engine	Rolls-Royce Derwent 5 3,500lb		Rolls-Royce Derwent 8 3,600lb	
Span	33ft	33ft	34ft 2in	34ft 2in
Length	30ft 6in	42ft 4in	42ft 4in	42ft 4in
Gross weight	8,600lb	9,500lb	9,800lb	10,000lb
Serial No	VX784	VX790	WD280, WZ736	WZ744

Below:
XA896 in all white anti-flash finish — the same paint was later used on Concorde. The large black underwing serials were replaced in the early 1960s by toned down pale blue fin serials and pale red and blue insignia.

— Vulcan Squadrons

VULCAN SQUADRONS

No 230 OCU   Formed Waddington July 1956 with Vulcan B.1, insignia — City of Lincoln coat of arms; Finningley June 1961, Vulcan B.1/B.2, insignia — white Yorkshire rose; Scampton December 1969, Vulcan B.2, insignia — yellow sword on blue and white disc. Disbanded 31 August 1981.

No 9 Squadron   Formed Coningsby 1 March 1962; Cottesmore November 1964; Akrotiri January 1969; Waddington January 1975; disbanded 30 April 1982. Vulcan B.2 throughout; insignia — a bat.

No 12 Squadron   Formed Coningsby 1 July 1962; Cottesmore November 1964; disbanded 31 December 1967. Vulcan B.2 throughout; insignia — fox's head.

No 27 Squadron   Formed Scampton 1 April 1961 with Vulcan B.2; disbanded 29 March 1972. Re-formed Scampton 1 November 1973 with Vulcan B.2/SR.2; disbanded 31 March 1982; insignia — an elephant.

No 35 Squadron   Formed Coningsby 1 November 1962; Cottesmore November 1964; Akrotiri January 1969; Scampton January 1975; disbanded 28 February 1982. Vulcan B.2 throughout; insignia — Pegasus flying horse and then numerals '35' joined together and called 'the Skyhook'.

No 44(R) Squadron   Formed Waddington 10 August 1960 with Vulcan B.1s; converted Vulcan B.2 1967; disbanded 31 December 1982; insignia — numerals '44'.

No 50 Squadron   Formed Waddington 1 August 1961 with Vulcan B.1; converted Vulcan B.2 1966-67; disbanded 31 March 1984; insignia — two running dingoes.

No 83 Squadron   Formed Waddington 21 May 1957 with Vulcan B.1; converted Vulcan B.2 November 1960; disbanded 29 August 1969; insignia — an antler.

No 101 Squadron   Formed Finningley 15 October 1957 with Vulcan B.1; Waddington June 1961; converted Vulcan B.2 1967; disbanded 4 August 1982; insignia — numerals '101' incorporating Squadron crest of lion in turret.

No 617 Squadron   Formed Scampton 1 May 1958 with Vulcan B.1; converted Vulcan B.2 September 1961; disbanded 31 December 1981; insignia — three lightning flashes, then breached dam on diamond background.

Below:
The original Vulcan low-level glossy polyurethane camouflage of dark green and medium sea grey. To minimise detection, the black serials have reappeared and the starboard roundel has been deleted. *BAe*

— Vulcan Production

Prototypes

Contract 6/Acft/1942/CB.6(a)

VX770 A&AEE for trials; engine test-bed; disintegrated at Syerston, Notts, 20 September 1958.

VX777 Aerodynamic test aircraft; converted to prototype B.2; last flew 27 April 1960; scrapped Farnborough 1963 — fuselage used for 'bombing-up' trials.

B.1 and B.1A

Contract 6/Acft/8442/CB.6(a). 25 off — 14 August 1952

1. XA889 A&AEE; Olympus development aircraft at Patchway 1957; scrapped Boscombe 1971.
2. XA890 RAE test aircraft — radio/radar trials aircraft; scrapped 1971.
3. XA891 Engine installation development aircraft, crashed at Walkington near Hull on 24 July 1959 when electrics failed.
4. XA892 A&AEE — armament trials aircraft; instructional airframe at Halton; scrapped 1972.
5. XA893 A&AEE — B.2 electrical trials; dismantled at Boscombe 1962.
6. XA894 A&AEE; Bristol Siddeley engine test bed. Modified to carry TSR.2 engine in ventral pod — burnt out when engine exploded during ground runs on 3 December 1962.
7. XA895 No 230 OCU, 19 January 1957; A&AEE for ECM trials; BCDU; converted to B.1A; withdrawn 13 January 1967; scrapped 19 September 1968.
8. XA896 No 230 OCU, 7 March 1957; No 83 Squadron; No 44 Squadron; No 230 OCU. Transferred to Ministry of Aviation June 1964 for trials with underslung vectored-thrust engine intended for Hawker P.1154 — when fighter scrapped, XA896 quickly followed suit.
9. XA897 Crashed London Airport 1 October 1956.
10. XA898 No 230 OCU, 3 January 1957; Halton instructional airframe, 26 August 1964; scrapped 1971.
11. XA899 A&AEE, 28 February 1957 — autopilot development aircraft; Cosford instructional airframe; scrapped 1973.
12. XA900 No 230 OCU, 25 March 1957; No 101 Squadron; No 230 OCU; Cosford instructional airframe, 28 February 1966; preserved.
13. XA901 No 230 OCU, 4 April 1957; No 83 Squadron; No 44 Squadron; Cranwell instructional airframe; scrapped 1972.
14. XA902 No 230 OCU, 10 May 1957; damaged in landing accident 28 February 1958; Rolls-Royce test bed; scrapped 1963.
15. XA903 A&AEE, 31 May 1957; RAE — Blue Steel trials; Concorde Olympus test bed; Tornado RB.199 test bed; finally landed as last airworthy B.1 on 22 February 1979; Farnborough fire dump.
16. XA904 No 83 Squadron, 16 July 1957; converted to B.1A 1960; No 44 Squadron; crash landed Waddington 1 March 1961 when ran out of fuel; instructional airframe.
17. XA905 No 83 Squadron, 11 July 1957; No 44 Squadron; No 230 OCU; Waddington Wing; Newton instructional airframe; scrapped 1974.
18. XA906 No 83 Squadron, 12 August 1957; No 44 Squadron; converted to B.1A 1962; Waddington Wing; stored at St Athan, 10 March 1967; scrapped 6 November 1968.
19. XA907 No 83 Squadron, 29 August 1957; No 44 Squadron; converted to B.1A 1961; Waddington Wing; BCDU; scrapped 20 May 1968.
20. XA908 No 83 Squadron, 17 September 1957; crashed near Detroit, 24 October 1958.
21. XA909 No 101 Squadron, 1 October 1957; converted to B.1A 1962; No 50 Squadron; Waddington Wing; crashed near Gwalchmai, Anglesey, 16 July 1964, after engine exploded — crew escaped.
22. XA910 No 101 Squadron, 1 November 1957; No 230 OCU; converted to B.1A 1962; No 50 Squadron; No 44 Squadron; scrapped.
23. XA911 No 83 Squadron, 1 November 1957; No 230 OCU; converted to B.1A 1962; Waddington Wing; engines blew-up in January 1964 but repaired; St Athan, 2 February 1967; scrapped 8 November 1968.
24. XA912 No 101 Squadron, 2 December 1957; converted to B.1A 1960; Waddington Wing; St Athan, 9 March 1967; scrapped 20 May 1968.
25. XA913 No 101 Squadron, 19 December 1957; converted to B.1A 1961; Waddington Wing; St Athan, 21 December 1966; scrapped 20 May 1968.

Above:
From 1973 onwards, the Vulcan finish was changed to matt camouflage colours and type 'B' roundels (red and blue only). XM575 has also reverted to carrying a roundel on each wing upper surface, though this practice was not universal throughout the force. Notice the 'squared-off' fin tip on this No 44 Squadron aircraft which housed the passive warning radar receiver aerial and which, after trials on XM597, appeared in service from 1975. *BAe*

Contract 6/Acft/11301/CB.6(a). 20 off —
30 September 1954

26. XH475 No 230 OCU, 22 January 1958; No 101 Squadron; converted to B.1A 1962; Waddington Wing; instructional airframe, 20 November 1967; scrapped 7 June 1969.
27. XH476 No 101 Squadron, 5 February 1958; converted to B.1A 1962; No 44 Squadron; Waddington Wing; withdrawn 4 May 1967; scrapped 21 January 1969.
28. XH477 No 83 Squadron, 18 February 1958; No 44 Squadron; converted to B.1A 1960; No 50 Squadron; crashed St Colm Hill, Aboyne, near Aberdeen, 12 June 1963 — crew killed.
29. XH478 Ministry of Aviation, 31 March 1958, to test flight refuelling probe; converted to B.1A; Waddington Wing; Akrotiri for ground training in March 1969.
30. XH479 No 101 Squadron, 28 March 1958; converted to B.1A 1961; Waddington Wing; Halton instructional airframe; scrapped 1973.
31. XH480 No 83 Squadron, 22 April 1958; No 44 Squadron; converted to B.1A 1962; Waddington Wing; St Athan, 10 November 1966; scrapped 30 September 1968.
32. XH481 No 101 Squadron, 30 April 1958; converted to B.1A 1960; Waddington Wing; Cottesmore fire dump, 11 January 1968; scrapped 1977.
33. XH482 No 617 Squadron, 5 May 1958; No 50

Squadron; converted B.1A 1962; No 101 Squadron; Waddington Wing; St Athan, 13 October 1966; scrapped 19 September 1968.
34. XH483 No 617 Squadron, 20 May 1958; converted B.1A 1961; No 50 Squadron; Waddington Wing; Manston fire dump, 3 August 1967; burnt 1977.
35. XH497 No 617 Squadron, 30 May 1958; No 50 Squadron; converted B.1A 1962; Waddington Wing; withdrawn 17 May 1966; scrapped 1969.
36. XH498 No 617 Squadron, 30 June 1958; No 50 Squadron; converted B.1A 1962; Waddington Wing; instructional airframe; scrapped.
37. XH499. No 617 Squadron, 18 July 1958; No 50 Squadron; converted B.1A 1962; No 44 Squadron; A&AEE; dismantled at Bitteswell November 1965.
38. XH500 No 617 Squadron, 15 August 1958; converted B.1A 1959; BCDU; No 50 Squadron; Waddington Wing; instructional airframe; burnt 1977.
39. XH501 No 617 Squadron, 3 September 1958; converted B.1A 1961; Nos 44/50 Squadrons; St Athan, 11 October 1966; scrapped 8 November 1968.
40. XH502 No 617 Squadron, 11 November 1958; No 50 Squadron; converted B.1A 1962; Waddington Wing; Scampton fire dump, January 1968; nose to Waddington crew escape-drill trainer.
41. XH503 No 83 Squadron, 31 December 1958; No 44 Squadron; converted B.1A 1962/63; Waddington Wing; St Athan, 6 December 1966; scrapped 8 November 1968.
42. XH504 No 230 OCU, 31 December 1958; converted B.1A 1961; Waddington Wing; withdrawn 4 January 1968; Cottesmore fire dump.
43. XH505 No 230 OCU, 13 March 1959; first conversion to B.1A 1959/60; No 617 Squadron; No 50 Squadron; Waddington Wing; Finningley fire dump 9 January 1968.
44. XH506 No 101 Squadron, 17 April 1959; converted B.1A 1960; No 617 Squadron; No 50 Squadron; Waddington Wing; scrapped 8 November 1968.
45. XH532 No 230 OCU, 31 March 1959; No 101 Squadron; converted B.1A 1962; Waddington Wing; withdrawn 17 May 1966; scrapped 8 November 1968.

B.2

Contract 6/Acft/11301/CB.6(a). 17 off —
30 September 1954

1. XH533 A&AEE, 26 March 1959; scrapped at St Athan 1970.

2. XH534   A&AEE, No 230 OCU, December 1966; converted to SR.2; No 27 Squadron; scrapped 16 February 1982.
3. XH535   A&AEE, 27 May 1960; crashed near Andover, 11 May 1964 — four rear crew killed.
4. XH536   A&AEE, 16 December 1959; Coningsby/Cottesmore Wing; crashed Wales, 11 February 1966 — all died.
5. XH537   A&AEE; Skybolt testbed; No 230 OCU in May 1965; Scampton Wing; Abingdon fire dump, 25 March 1982.
6. XH538   A&AEE/Avro; Blue Steel and Skybolt testbed; No 230 OCU; No 27 Squadron; Waddington Wing; No 35 Squadron; scrapped 31 August 1981.
7. XH539   A&AEE/Avro; Blue Steel testbed; Waddington fire dump, 7 March 1972.
8. XH554   No 83 Squadron, 7 April 1961; No 230 OCU; Scampton Wing; Catterick fire dump 9 June 1981.
9. XH555   No 27 Squadron, 14 July 1961; No 230 OCU; damaged beyond repair during heavy landing at Finningley in 1968; fatigue trials at Woodford; cut-up for structural integrity tests in 1971.
10. XH556   No 27 Squadron, 29 September 1961; No 230 OCU; undercarriage collapsed on start-up of engines at Finningley on 18 April 1966 — scrapped.
11. XH557.   Bristol Siddeley; Cottesmore Wing, 3 December 1965; Waddington Wing; NEAF Wing; Waddington Wing; scrapped December 1982.
12. XH558   No 230 OCU, 1 July 1960; Waddington Wing; No 50 Squadron; converted to B.2(K).
13. XH559   No 230 OCU, August 1960; scrapped St Athan May 1981.
14. XH560   No 230 OCU, 1 October 1960; No 12 Squadron; No 230 OCU; No 27 Squadron; No 50 Squadron; converted to B.2(K).
15. XH561   No 230 OCU, November 1960; landed with undercarriage selected up, 15 January 1965; No 50 Squadron; converted to B.2(K).

Below:
'Red Flag' experience showed that the white underside of the Vulcan exposed it to fighters in tight turns. Beginning with XM657 in September 1979, Vulcans which underwent major servicing returned in a new overall camouflage scheme of matt dark green and dark grey, both top and bottom.

16. XH562 No 230 OCU, 8 December 1960; No 35 Squadron; No 44 Squadron; No 230 OCU; No 101 Squadron; No 50 Squadron; Catterick crash rescue training airframe, 19 August 1982.
17. XH563 No 83 Squadron, 23 December 1960; No 12 Squadron; A&AEE for Skybolt electrical system tests; No 230 OCU; converted SR.2; No 27 Squadron; withdrawn 5 April 1982; Scampton 'gate guardian'.

Contract 6/Acft/11830/CB.6(a). Eight off — 31 March 1955

18. XJ780 No 83 Squadron, 13 January 1961; No 12 Squadron; No 230 OCU; converted to SR.2; No 27 Squadron; scrapped November 1982.
19. XJ781 No 83 Squadron, 22 February 1961; No 12 Squadron; No 230 OCU; Waddington Wing; NEAF Wing; crash landed Shiraz, Iran, with port undercarriage locked up, 23 May 1973.
20. XJ782 No 83 Squadron, 1 March 1961; No 12 Squadron; No 230 OCU; No 44 Squadron; Finningley 'gate guardian' 4 September 1982.
21. XJ783 No 83 Squadron, 10 March 1961; No 9 Squadron; NEAF Wing; No 617 Squadron; No 35 Squadron; No 101 Squadron; scrapped November 1982.
22. XJ784 A&AEE; No 230 OCU, 21 December 1966; No 9 Squadron; No 50 Squadron; No 9 Squadron; No 101 Squadron; scrapped December 1982.
23. XJ823 No 27 Squadron, 20 April 1961; No 35 Squadron; No 230 OCU; Waddington Wing; NEAF Wing; No 27 Squadron; No 35 Squadron; Waddington Wing; withdrawn 21 January 1983; on display in Carlisle.
24. XJ824 No 27 Squadron, 15 May 1961; No 230 OCU; No 9 Squadron; NEAF Wing; No 101 Squadron; to Duxford 13 March 1982 for preservation in Imperial War Museum collection.
25. XJ825 No 27 Squadron, 27 July 1961; No 9 Squadron; No 12 Squadron; No 35 Squadron; No 50 Squadron; converted to B.2(K).

Contract 6/Acft/13145/CB.6(a). 24 off — 25 February 1956

26. XL317 Ministry of Aviation; 617 Squadron, 7 June 1962; retired to Akrotiri 1 December 1981.
27. XL318 No 617 Squadron, 1 September 1961; No 230 OCU; No 617 Squadron; on display in Gibraltar.
28. XL319 No 617 Squadron, 20 October 1961; No 83 Squadron; Scampton Wing; No 44 Squadron; displayed at Sunderland Airport.
29. XL320 No 617 Squadron, 1 December 1961; Scampton Wing; 230 OCU; No 617 Squadron; No 230 OCU; scrapped 31 August 1981.
30. XL321 No 617 Squadron, 10 January 1962; No 230 OCU; No 35 Squadron; Scampton Wing; No 44 Squadron; No 50 Squadron; 6,996 flying hours — largest total in any Vulcan; Catterick for rescue training, 19 September 1982.
31. XL359 No 617 Squadron, 1 February 1962; No 230 OCU; No 35 Squadron; Scampton Wing; Scampton fire dump March 1982; scrapped November 1982.
32. XL360 No 617 Squadron, 1 March 1962; Scampton Wing; No 35 Squadron; No 230 OCU; No 44 Squadron; Midlands Air Museum, Coventry, on 26 January 1982.
33. XL361 No 617 Squadron, 14 March 1962; A&AEE; Scampton Wing; No 35 Squadron; Waddington Wing; written off at Goose Bay 21 December 1981.
34. XL384 No 230 OCU, March 1962; Scampton Wing; 'Window' trials aircraft; No 27 Squadron; No 617 Squadron; No 230 OCU; scrapped 1 January 1975 after heavy landing.
35. XL385 No 9 Squadron, 17 April 1962; Scampton Wing; 1 and 2 engines blew up on take-off on 6 April 1967 — burnt out.
36. XL386 No 9 Squadron, 11 May 1962; No 83 Squadron; No 44 Squadron; No 101 Squadron; No 44 Squadron; Manston for crash rescue training 26 August 1982.
37. XL387 No 230 OCU, 1 June 1962; Waddington Wing; Scampton Wing; No 50 Squadron; scrapped 15 December 1982.
38. XL388 No 9 Squadron, 13 June 1962 — christened 'Mayflower III' when made goodwill visit to USA in conjunction with sailing of replica of Pilgrim Fathers' ship; No 83 Squadron; Scampton Wing; No 44 Squadron; Honington for fire practice on 2 April 1982.
39. XL389 No 230 OCU, 11 July 1962; No 617 Squadron; No 9 Squadron; Scampton Wing; No 101 Squadron; scrapped.
40. XL390 No 9 Squadron, 19 July 1962; Scampton Wing; No 617 Squadron; crashed near Glenview Naval Air Station, Chicago, while practising for display on 12 August 1978 — crew killed.
41. XL391 A&AEE; BCDU, 22 May 1963; Nos 9/35 Squadrons; No 44 Squadron; No 101 Squadron; Blackpool Airport for preservation on 16 February 1983.
42. XL392 No 83 Squadron, 1 August 1962; Scampton Wing; No 35 Squadron; RAF Valley fire dump 24 March 1982.
43. XL425 No 83 Squadron, 30 August 1982; Scampton Wing; scrapped 13 April 1982.
44. XL426 No 83 Squadron, 12 September 1962;

Above:
**Like the Victor tanker, the Vulcan B.2(K) had much of
the underside painted in white with a longitudinal
red-and-black bar to assist alignment by an
approaching receiver.** *Crown Copyright*

Scampton Wing; No 50 Squadron; still flying
as display aircraft.

45. XL427 No 83 Squadron, 1 October 1962;
Scampton Wing; No 44 Squadron; Macri-
hanish for fire practice 13 August 1982.

46. XL443. No 83 Squadron, 5 October 1962;
Scampton Wing; NEAF Wing; No 35 Squadron; scrapped June 1982.

47. XL444 No 27 Squadron, 30 October 1962;
Scampton Wing; No 230 OCU; No 617 Squadron; No 230 OCU; No 35 Squadron; Waddington Wing; scrapped December 1982.

48. XL445 No 27 Squadron, 24 November 1962;
Scampton Wing; NEAF Wing — ran off
runway due to loss of hydraulics 1969; No 230
OCU; No 35 Squadron; No 44 Squadron;
No 50 Squadron; converted to B.2(K).

49. XL446 No 27 Squadron, 29 November 1962;
Waddington Wing; No 230 OCU; NEAF
Wing; Waddington Wing; No 617 Squadron;
scrapped November 1982.

*Contract KD/B/01/CB.6(a). 40 off — 22 January
1958*

50. XM569 No 27 Squadron, 31 January 1963;
Waddington Wing; Cottesmore Wing; No 27
Squadron; Waddington Wing; No 44 Squad-
ron; Wales Aircraft Museum 21 January 1983.

51. XM570 No 27 Squadron, 26 February 1963;
No 617 Squadron; scrapped 29 January 1982.

52. XM571 No 83 Squadron, 21 February 1963;
Scampton Wing; No 50 Squadron; converted
to B.2(K).

53. XM572 No 83 Squadron, 1 March 1963;
Waddington Wing; No 617 Squadron; scrapped November 1982.

54. XM573 No 83 Squadron, 27 March 1963;

No 230 OCU; No 44 Squadron; presented to
SAC Museum, Offutt, 16 June 1982.

55. XM574 No 27 Squadron, 17 June 1963;
Scampton Wing; scrapped 29 January 1982.

56. XM575 No 617 Squadron, 21 May 1963;
Scampton Wing; Waddington Wing; No 44
Squadron; Leicester Air Museum 25 January
1983.

57. XM576 No 27 Squadron, June 1963; Scampton Wing; crashed on landing at Scampton 25
May 1965 — scrapped.

58. XM594 No 27 Squadron, 9 July 1963;
Scampton Wing; No 44 Squadron; Newark Air
Museum 19 January 1983.

59. XM595 No 617 Squadron, 20 August 1963;
Scampton Wing; No 617 Squadron; No 35
Squadron; scrapped November 1982.

60. XM596 Aircraft not completed — fatigue
test specimen.

61. XM597 No 12 Squadron, 27 August 1963;
Waddington Wing; No 35 Squadron; No 50
Squadron; No 9 Squadron; No 101 Squadron;
No 35 Squadron.

62. XM598 No 12 Squadron, 3 September
1963; No 44 Squadron; Cosford Aerospace
Museum 20 January 1983.

63. XM599 No 35 Squadron, 30 September
1963; No 44 Squadron; Waddington Wing; No
2 engine blew back and extensive fire on
take-off — April 1976; scrapped 29 January
1982.

64. XM600 No 35 Squadron, 2 October 1963;
Cottesmore Wing; Waddington Wing; engine
bay fire, 17 January 1977, crashed 10 miles east
of Coningsby — crew baled out.

65. XM601 No 9 Squadron, 4 November 1963;
crashed on landing at Coningsby, 7 October
1964 — crew killed.

66. XM602 No 12 Squadron, 12 November 1963;
No 101 Squadron; St Athan Air Museum
16 March 1983.

67. XM603 No 9 Squadron, 3 December 1963;
Coningsby/Cottesmore Wing; Waddington

Wing; No 101 Squadron; No 44 Squadron; Woodford for preservation 12 March 1982.

68. XM604 No 35 Squadron, 4 December 1963; Coningsby/Cottesmore Wing; crashed Cow Close Farm on overshoot from Cottesmore, 30 January 1968.

69. XM605 No 9 Squadron, 20 December 1963; Coningsby/Cottesmore Wing; Waddington Wing; No 50 Squadron; presented to USAF Museum, Castle AFB, California, 8 September 1981.

70. XM606 No 12 Squadron, 20 December 1963; Coningsby/Cottesmore Wing; A&AEE for TFR trials; Waddington Wing; 8th Air Force Museum, Barksdale, Louisiana, 9 June 1982.

71. XM607 No 35 Squadron, 31 December 1963; No 101 Squadron; No 44 Squadron; Waddington 'gate guardian'.

72. XM608 No 9 Squadron, 28 January 1964; Coningsby/Cottesmore Wing; Waddington Wing; No 1 engine blew up on take-off, 6 December 1976 — repaired; retired March 1981; scrapped December 1982.

73. XM609 No 12 Squadron, 28 January 1964; Coningsby/Cottesmore Wing; Waddington Wing; retired March 1981; scrapped 31 August 1981.

74. XM610 No 9 Squadron, 11 February 1964; Coningsby/Cottesmore Wing; Waddington Wing; sank through hangar floor at Goose Bay, 17 January 1969; crashed Wingate, Co Durham, 8 January 1971 after engine fire. Crew baled out.

75. XM611 No 9 Squadron, 13 February 1964; Coningsby/Cottesmore Wing; Waddington Wing; retired 28 January 1982; scrapped.

76. XM612 No 9 Squadron, 2 March 1964; Coningsby/Cottesmore Wing; Waddington Wing; No 44 Squadron; City of Norwich Aviation Museum 30 January 1983.

77. XM645 Coningsby/Cottesmore Wing, 11 March 1964; Waddington Wing; No 230 OCU; Waddington Wing; No 35 Squadron; No 9 Squadron; blew up over Malta after heavy landing, 14 October 1975 — rear crew killed.

78. XM646 No 12 Squadron, 7 April 1964; Coningsby/Cottesmore Wing; NEAF Wing; Waddington Wing; retired 26 January 1982; scrapped.

79. XM647 No 35 Squadron, 15 April 1964; Coningsby/Cottesmore Wing; NEAF Wing; Waddington Wing; No 44 Squadron; Laarbruch fire dump 17 September 1982.

80. XM648 No 9 Squadron, 5 May 1964; No 101 Squadron; No 44 Squadron; scrapped December 1982.

81. XM649 No 9 Squadron, 13 May 1964; Coningsby/Cottesmore Wing; Waddington Wing; scrapped 2 December 1982.

82. XM650 No 12 Squadron, 27 May 1964; Waddington Wing; scrapped 16 March 1983.

83. XM651 No 12 Squadron, 19 June 1964; No 50 Squadron; scrapped November 1982.

84. XM652 No 9 Squadron, 14 August 1964; No 44 Squadron; No 35 Squadron; No 50 Squadron.

85. XM653 No 9 Squadron, 3 September 1964; Waddington Wing; retired 18 December 1980; scrapped 28 July 1981.

86. XM654 No 12 Squadron, 22 October 1964; No 101 Squadron; Waddington Wing; No 35 Squadron; scrapped December 1982.

87. XM655 No 9 Squadron, 20 November 1964; No 44 Squadron; No 50 Squadron; No 101 Squadron; No 44 Squadron.

88. XM656 No 35 Squadron, 14 December 1964; Coningsby/Cottesmore Wing; Waddington Wing; No 35 Squadron; scrapped 30 March 1983.

89. XM657 No 35 Squadron, December 1964; No 44 Squadron; Waddington Wing; Manston fire dump 5 January 1982.

Notes: For security reasons, details of Vulcan B.2 squadron usage not necessarily complete. During the era of centralised servicing, aircraft belonged to a wing rather than a squadron.

Selected Bibliography

Brookes, Andrew, *V-Force*, Jane's 1982.

Clark, Ronald W. *The Role of the Bomber*, Sidgwick & Jackson, 1977.

Davies, S. D., 'The History of the Avro Vulcan', *The Aeronautical Journal*, May 1970.

English, Malcolm, 'Operation Black Buck', *Air Pictorial*, July 1983.

Ethell, J. & Price, A. *Air War South Atlantic*, Sidgwick & Jackson, 1983.

Francis, Hugh, 'Blue Steel, 53rd Lecture, The Royal Aeronautical Society, 6 November 1963.

Goulding, J. & Moyes, P., *RAF Bomber Command and its Aircraft 1936-40, 1941-45*, Ian Allan 1975 and 1978.

Hardy, M. J., *Avro*, Patrick Stephens, 1982.

HMSO, *The Malayan Emergency 1948/1960*, 1970.

Jackson, A. J., *Avro Aircraft since 1908*, Putnam, 1965.

Jackson, Paul A., 'The Voluptuous Vulcan', *Aviation News*, Vol 8, No 25, May 1980.

Lewis, Peter, *The British Bomber since 1914*, Putnam.

Rees, Elfan ap, 'Avro Vulcan', *Air Pictorial*, May and June 1974.

Smith, David J., *Action Stations — Wales and the North West*, Patrick Stephens, 1981.

Taylor, J. W., *The Avro Vulcan*, Aircraft Profiles.